Jon Sachs

About the Author

Ross W. Greene, Ph.D., is Associate Clinical Professor in the Department of Psychiatry at Harvard Medical School and the originator of Collaborative Problem Solving, an approach for helping kids with social, emotional, and behavioral challenges. He consults extensively with families, general and special education schools, inpatient and residential facilities, and systems of juvenile detention, and lectures widely throughout the world. Dr. Greene lives near Boston with his wife and two children.

The
Explosive
Child

Funded by
MISSION COLLEGE
Carl D. Perkins Vocational and Technical Education Act Grant

The
Explosive
Child

A New Approach for Understanding
and Parenting Easily Frustrated,
Chronically Inflexible Children

ROSS W. GREENE, PH.D.

HARPER

NEW YORK • LONDON • TORONTO • SYDNEY

HARPER

THE EXPLOSIVE CHILD. Copyright © 1998, 2001, 2005, 2010 by Ross W. Greene. All rights reserved. Printed in the United States of America. No part of this book may be used or reproduced in any manner whatsoever without written permission except in the case of brief quotations embodied in critical articles and reviews. For information address HarperCollins Publishers, 10 East 53rd Street, New York, NY 10022.

HarperCollins books may be purchased for educational, business, or sales promotional use. For information please write: Special Markets Department, HarperCollins Publishers, 10 East 53rd Street, New York, NY 10022.

First Harper paperback published 2005. Reset 2010.

Designed by Phil Mazzone

Library of Congress Cataloging-in-Publication Data is available upon request.

ISBN 978-0-06-190619-0

11 12 13 14   OV/RRD   10 9 8 7 6 5

In memory of Irving A. Greene

Anyone can become angry, that is easy. . .
but to be angry with the right person, to the right degree,
at the right time, for the right purpose, and in the right
way . . . this is not easy.   **—Aristotle**

If I am not for myself, who is for me?
If I am only for myself, what am I?
If not now, when?   **—Hillel**

Illusions are the truths we live by until we know better.
                                     —Nancy Gibbs

Contents

Preface   xi

Acknowledgments   xv

1   The Waffle Episode   1

2   Kids Do Well If They Can   11

3   Lagging Skills and Unsolved Problems   21

4   Drama in Real Life   49

5   The Truth About Consequences   71

6   Three Plans (One in Particular)   83

7   Trouble in Paradise   119

8   B Scenes   151

9   Extra Help   175

10 Family Matters   221

11 The Dinosaur in the Building   251

12 Better   289

    Additional Reading   295

    Index   299

Preface

Welcome to the fourth edition of *The Explosive Child*, which comes twelve years after the first edition was published in 1998. One of the exciting things about the approach to helping challenging kids—called Collaborative Problem Solving—described in these pages is that it continues to evolve as I try to make it as clear and accessible as possible for the adults who live and work with kids with behavioral challenges. This edition reflects the most current updates to the model.

Often people ask, "How do I know if my child is explosive?" There's no blood test, of course. "Explosive" is a metaphor for kids who become frustrated far more easily, far more often, and in ways that are far more extreme—screaming, swearing, spitting, hitting, kicking, biting, cutting, destroying property—than "ordinary" kids. These are the kids who are pushed beyond the brink far more easily and respond far less adaptively and flexibly than most. While the title of this book suggests that it is only about the kids who explode, it's applicable to kids who are exhibiting any variety of challenging behaviors.

Challenging kids have, of course, been described in many ways: difficult, willful, manipulative, attention-seeking, limit-testing, contrary, intransigent, unmotivated. They may carry various psychiatric diagnoses, such as oppositional-defiant disorder (ODD), bipolar disorder, attention-deficit/hyperactivity disorder (ADHD), intermittent explosive disorder, Tourette's disorder, depression, reactive-attachment disorder, nonverbal learning disability, Asperger's disorder, and obsessive-compulsive disorder (OCD). While these diagnoses can be useful in some ways—perhaps especially if the goal is to help people take a kid's behavioral challenges seriously—they aren't very useful at helping people understand their challenges or know what to do about them.

For a long time the prevailing view was that kids' challenging behavior is the by-product of passive, permissive, inconsistent, noncontingent parenting practices. But we've learned a lot about challenging kids in the past thirty years, and the research suggests that the difficulties of challenging kids are a lot more complex than previously thought. We need to be sure that what we do to help challenging kids reflects what we now know about them.

In writing this and the earlier editions of *The Explosive Child*, my goal has been to provide an enlightened understanding of these kids and, flowing from this understanding, to describe a practical, comprehensive approach aimed at decreasing adversarial interactions between challenging kids and their adult caregivers and improving these children's capacities for flexibility, frustration tolerance, communication, problem solving, conflict resolution, and self-regulation.

As always, the only prerequisite is an open mind.

Ross W. Greene, Ph.D.
Boston, Massachusetts

Acknowledgments

My thinking about how to help challenging kids and their adult caregivers interact more adaptively has been influenced by many parents, teachers, and supervisors. It was my incredible good fortune to have been mentored by Dr. Thomas Ollendick while I was a graduate student in the clinical psychology program at Virginia Tech. Two psychologists who supervised me during my training years were particularly influential: Drs. George Clum at Virginia Tech and Mary Ann McCabe at Children's National Medical Center in Washington, D.C. A social worker named Lorraine Lougee gets credit for teaching me not to be shy about taking a strong stand on behalf of kids who need help. And I probably wouldn't have gone into psychology in the first place if I hadn't stumbled across the path of Dr. Elizabeth Altmaier when I was an undergraduate at the University of Florida. Many theorists and researchers have also influenced my thinking. While it's not possible to mention each one, Walter Mischel, George Kelly, and Grazyna Kochanska come to mind in particular.

However, those who were most central to the evolution of many of the ideas in this book, and to whom I owe the greatest debt of gratitude, were the many kids, parents, educators, and staff with whom I've had the pleasure of working over the years.

I also want to acknowledge the countless people throughout the world who have embraced the Collaborative Problem Solving approach and, against the odds but with vision and energy and relentless determination, have advocated for implementation of the approach in their schools, clinics, inpatient units, and residential and juvenile detention facilities. There are truly amazing people in this world who care deeply about improving the lives of kids, and I have been privileged to have crossed paths with many of you.

This book is about children and families, and I'd be remiss if I didn't acknowledge my own: my wife, Melissa; my kids, Talia and Jacob, who keep me laughing and learning and make sure I practice what I preach; and Sandy, the Big Black Dog.

While there are many girls who exhibit challenging behavior, for ease of exposition most of this book is written in the masculine gender. Also, while I try to use "people first" phraseology whenever possible, I do use "explosive child" and "explosive kid" interchangeably throughout. The names and identifying information of all the children in this book are completely fictitious. Any resemblance to actual children of the same names is, as the saying goes, purely coincidental.

The
Explosive
Child

1

The Waffle Episode

Jennifer, age eleven, wakes up, makes her bed, looks around her room to make sure everything is in its place, and heads into the kitchen to make herself breakfast. She peers into the freezer, removes the container of frozen waffles, and counts six waffles. Thinking to herself, "I'll have three waffles this morning and three tomorrow morning," Jennifer toasts her three waffles and sits down to eat.

Moments later, her mother and five-year-old brother, Adam, enter the kitchen, and the mother asks Adam what he'd like to eat for breakfast. Adam responds, "Waffles," and the mother reaches into the freezer for the waffles. Jennifer, who has been listening intently, explodes.

"He can't have the frozen waffles!" Jennifer screams, her face suddenly reddening.

"Why not?" asks her mother, her voice rising, at a loss for an explanation of Jennifer's behavior.

"I was going to have those waffles tomorrow morning!" Jennifer screams, jumping out of her chair.

"I'm not telling your brother he can't have waffles!" her mother yells back.

"He can't have them!" screams Jennifer, now face to face with her mother.

The mother, wary of the physical and verbal aggression of which her daughter is capable during these moments, desperately asks Adam if there might be something else he would consider eating.

"I want waffles," whimpers Adam, cowering behind his mother.

Jennifer, her frustration and agitation at a peak, pushes her mother out of the way, seizes the container of frozen waffles, then slams the freezer door shut, pushes over a kitchen chair, grabs her plate of toasted waffles, and stalks to her room. Her brother and mother begin to cry.

Jennifer's family members have endured literally hundreds of such explosions. In many instances, the explosions are more prolonged and intense and involve more physical or verbal aggression than the one described above (when Jennifer was eight, she kicked out a window in the family car). Doctors have bestowed myriad diagnoses on Jennifer: oppositional-defiant disorder, bipolar disorder, intermittent explosive disorder. For Jennifer's parents, however, a simple label doesn't begin to capture the upheaval, turmoil, and trauma that her outbursts cause . . . and doesn't help them understand their daughter or how best to help her.

Her siblings and mother are scared of her. Her extreme volatility and inflexibility require constant vigilance and enormous energy from her mother and father, consuming attention the parents wish they could devote to Jennifer's brother and sister. Her parents frequently argue over the best way to handle her behavior, but both agree about the severe strain Jennifer places on their marriage. Jennifer has no close friends; children who initially befriend her eventually find her rigid personality difficult to tolerate.

Over the years, Jennifer's parents have sought help from countless mental health professionals, most of whom have advised them to set firmer limits and be more consistent in managing Jennifer's behavior, and have instructed them on how to implement formal reward and punishment strategies, usually in the form of sticker charts and time-outs. When such strategies failed to work, Jennifer was medicated with multiple combinations of drugs, without dramatic effect. After eight years of disparate advice, firmer limits, motivational programs, and medicine, Jennifer has changed little since she was a toddler, when her parents first noticed there was something "different" about her. In fact, her outbursts are more intense and more frequent than ever.

"Most people can't imagine how humiliating it is to be scared of your own daughter," Jennifer's mother once said. "People who don't have a child like Jennifer don't have a clue about what it's like to live like this. Believe me, this is not what I envisioned when I dreamed of having children. This is a nightmare.

"You can't imagine the embarrassment of having Jennifer 'lose it' around people who don't know her," her mother continued. "I feel like telling them, 'I have two kids at home who don't act like this—I really am a good parent!'

"I know people are thinking, 'What wimpy parents she must have . . . what that kid really needs is a good thrashing.' Believe me, we've tried everything with her. But nobody's been able to tell us how to help her . . . no one's really been able to tell us what's the matter with her!

"I hate what I've become. I used to think of myself as a kind, patient, sympathetic person. But Jennifer has caused me to act in ways in which I never thought myself capable. I'm emotionally spent. I can't keep living like this.

"I know a lot of other parents who have pretty difficult children . . . you know, kids who are hyperactive or having trouble paying attention. I would give my left arm for a kid who was just hyperactive or having trouble paying attention! Jennifer is in a completely different league! It makes me feel very alone."

The truth is, Jennifer's mother is not alone; there are a lot of Jennifers out there. Their parents often discover that strategies that are usually effective for shaping the behavior of other children—such as explaining, reasoning, reassuring, nurturing, redirecting, insisting, ignoring, rewarding, and punishing—don't achieve the same success with their Jennifers. Even commonly prescribed medications often do not lead to satisfactory improvement. If you started reading this book because you have a Jennifer of your own, you're probably familiar with how frustrated, confused, angry, bitter, guilty, overwhelmed, worn-out, and hopeless Jennifer's parents feel.

Children like Jennifer are distinguished by a few characteristics—namely, striking inflexibility, low frustration tolerance, and poor problem-solving skills—that make life significantly more difficult and challenging for them and for the people who interact with them. These children have enormous difficulty thinking things through when they become frustrated and often respond to even simple changes and requests with extreme rigidity and verbal or physical aggression. For ease of exposition, I'll refer to these children throughout this book as "explosive," but the approach described in this book is applicable to kids who exhibit any variety of challenging behaviors.

How are explosive children different from other kids? Let's take a look at how different children may respond to a fairly common family scenario. Imagine that Child 1—Michael—is watching television, and his mother asks him to set the table for dinner. Michael has a pretty easy time shifting from his agenda—watching television—to his mother's agenda—setting the table for dinner. Thus, in response to "Michael, I'd like you to turn off the television and come set the table for dinner," he would likely reply, "Okay, Mom, I'm coming," and would set about the task of fulfilling his mother's request.

Child 2—Jermaine—is a little tougher. He has a harder time shifting from his agenda to his mother's agenda but is able to manage his frustration and shift gears (sometimes with the assistance of a threat hanging over his head). Thus, in response to "Jermaine, I'd like you to turn off the television and come set the table for dinner," Jermaine might initially shout, "No way, I don't want to right now!" or complain, "You always ask me to do things right when I'm in the middle of something I like!" However, with some extra help (Mother: "Jermaine, if you don't turn off the television and come set the dinner table right now, you're going to have to take a time-out"), these "somewhat tougher" children do shift gears.

And then there is Jennifer, Child 3, the explosive child, for whom shifting gears—from her agenda to her mother's agenda—often induces a fairly rapid, intense, debilitating level of frustration. In response to "Jennifer, I'd like you to turn off the television and come set the table for dinner," all bets are off on what she may say or do.

Explosive children come in all shapes and sizes. Some blow up dozens of times every day; others, only a few times a week. Many "lose it" only at home; others, only at school; still others, in both settings.

One such child, Richard, a spunky, charismatic fourteen-year-old who was diagnosed with ADHD, began to cry in our first session when I asked if he thought it might be a good idea for us to help him start managing his frustration so he could begin getting along better with his family members. Another, Jack—an engaging, smart, moody ten-year-old, who was diagnosed with bipolar disorder—had a very reliable pattern of becoming inflexible and irrational over the most trivial matters; his swearing and screaming in the midst of frustration tended to elicit similar behaviors from his parents. Still another, Marvin—a bright, active, impulsive, edgy, easily agitated eight-year-old who was diagnosed with Tourette's disorder, depression, and ADHD—reacted to unexpected changes with unimaginable intensity (and occasionally physical violence). On one occasion, Marvin's father innocently turned off an unnecessary light in the room in which Marvin was playing a video game, prompting a massive one-hour blowup.

What should become quite clear as you read this book is that these children have wonderful qualities and tremendous potential. In many ways, their general cognitive skills have developed at a usual pace. Yet their inflexibility, poor tolerance for frustration, and difficulty solving problems often obscure their more positive traits and cause them and those around them enormous pain. I can think of no other group of children who are so misunderstood. Their parents are typically caring, well-intentioned people who often feel guilty that they haven't been able to help their children.

"You know," Jennifer's mother would say, "each time I start to get my hopes up . . . each time I have a pleasant interaction with Jennifer . . . I let myself become a little optimistic and start to like her again . . . and then it all comes crashing down with her next explosion. I'm ashamed to say it, but a lot of the time I really don't like her, and I definitely don't like what she's doing to our family. We are in a perpetual state of crisis."

Clearly, there's something different about the Jennifers of the world. This is a critical realization for parents and others to come to. But there is hope, as long as their parents, teachers, relatives, and therapists are able to come to grips with a second realization: explosive children often require a different approach to discipline and limit-setting than do other children.

Dealing more effectively with explosive children requires, first and foremost, an *understanding* of why these children behave as they do. Once this understanding is achieved, strategies for helping things improve often become self-evident. In some instances, achieving a more accurate understanding of a child's difficulties can, by itself, lead to improvements in adult-child interactions, even before any formal strategies are tried. The first chapters of this book are devoted to helping you understand why these kids adapt so poorly to changes and requests, are so easily frustrated, and explode so quickly and so often. Along the way, you'll learn why popular strategies for dealing with difficult children may be less effective than expected. In later chapters, you'll read about alternative strategies that have been helpful to many of the children, families, and teachers with whom I've worked over the years.

If you are the parent of an explosive child, this book may restore some sanity to your family and help you feel that you can actually handle your child's difficulties confidently and competently. If you are a teacher, relative, friend, or therapist, this book should, at the least, help you understand. There is no panacea. But there is certainly cause for optimism and hope.

2

Kids Do Well If They Can

One of the most amazing and gratifying things about being a parent is watching your child develop new skills and master increasingly complex tasks with each passing month and year. Crawling progresses to walking and then advances to running; babbling slowly develops into full-blown talking; smiling progresses to more sophisticated forms of socialization; learning the letters of the alphabet sets the stage for reading whole words, then sentences, paragraphs, and books.

It goes without saying that different kids develop these and a host of other skills at vastly different paces. And development is often uneven within the same child;

for example, some children learn to read more readily than they learn to do addition and subtraction. When kids don't learn a skill as quickly or easily as expected, sometimes it's because they haven't been exposed to the material (for instance, maybe Steve can't hit a baseball very well because no one ever showed him how to do it). More common, kids have difficulty learning a particular skill even though they have the desire to master it and have been provided with the instruction typically needed to do so. It's not that they don't *want* to learn; it is simply that they are not learning as readily as expected. When this happens, we often give them special help (for example, providing remedial assistance in math or special instruction in hitting a baseball).

Just as some kids lag in acquiring certain academic or athletic skills, others—the kids this book is about—lag in some other very crucial skill areas: *flexibility, frustration tolerance,* and *problem solving.* Interacting well with other people and handling life's challenges without falling apart requires adaptability, proficiency in solving problems, the ability to resolve disagreements amicably, and modulating the emotions one experiences when frustrated. There aren't many situations in a kid's day that *don't* require flexibility, frustration tolerance, and problem solving. When two kids disagree about which game to play, we hope both kids possess the skills to resolve the dispute in a mutually satisfactory manner. When bad weather forces parents to cancel their child's much-anticipated trip to the amusement park, we hope the child has the ability to express his disappointment appropriately, consider alternative arrangements, and settle on a new plan. When a kid is engrossed in a video game and it's time to come to dinner, we hope the kid is able to interrupt his game, manage his understandable feelings of frustration, and think clearly enough to recognize that he can return to the game at a later time. And when a kid decides she'll have three frozen waffles for breakfast today and three tomorrow but her younger brother decides that he, too, wants waffles today, we hope the kid can move beyond inflexible thinking ("I am definitely going to have those three waffles for breakfast tomorrow, so there's no way my brother can have them") and come to a more flexible, adaptable, mutually satisfactory solution ("I guess I don't have to eat those exact waffles. I can ask Mom to buy more. Anyway, I might not even feel like eating waffles tomorrow.").

Some kids—those often referred to as having difficult temperaments—are inflexible and easily frustrated from the moment they pop into the world. As infants, they may be colicky and difficult to comfort or soothe, have irregular sleep patterns, have difficulties with feeding, and overreact to noises, lights, and discomfort (hunger, cold, a wet diaper, etc.). In other kids, difficulties with flexibility, frustration tolerance, and problem solving may not become apparent until later in childhood, when demands for increasingly complex social and communication skills, controlling impulses, and modulating emotions are heightened.

Here's the important point: the kids about whom this book is written do not *choose* to explode any more than a child would choose to have a reading disability. These kids lack crucial skills required for handling life's challenges. There's a big difference between viewing these kids' explosions as the result of the failure to progress developmentally and interpreting them as planned, intentional, and purposeful.

If you've been inclined or persuaded to embrace the latter view, then you're probably well versed in the conventional labels used to describe these kids, such as stubborn, willful, intransigent, manipulative, bratty, attention-seeking, spoiled, controlling, resistant, unmotivated, out of control, and defiant. And if you're the parent of one of these kids, you're also probably accustomed to being blamed for your child's explosive behavior. You see, the common assumption—even among many well-intentioned mental health professionals—is that kids are explosive because their parents are passive, permissive, inconsistent disciplinarians. Of course, this assumption doesn't take into account that many of the siblings of explosive children are actually very well behaved, and that many well-behaved kids have parents who are inconsistent disciplinarians. But, as you'd expect, this assumption leads to conventional strategies aimed at *making kids do well* and *teaching them who's boss* by helping their parents be firmer, more consistent disciplinarians, typically through implementation of popular programs involving sticker charts and point systems, rewards (such as special privileges) and punishments (such as time-outs and grounding). If you've found that this assumption and its associated labels and strategies haven't led to a productive outcome with your child, you are not alone.

Throughout this book, I encourage you to put the conventional wisdom to rest and consider the alternative view: that your child is already very motivated to do well and that his explosions reflect a developmental delay—a learning disability of sorts—in the skills of flexibility, frustration tolerance, and problem solving. From this perspective, focusing your energy on rewarding and punishing your child and teaching him who's the boss may actually be counterproductive because such an approach often sets the stage for explosions and won't teach him the skills he's lacking.

The single most important theme of this book is the title of this chapter: *kids do well if they can*. The basic premise of this theme is that if your kid *could* do well, he *would* do well. Doing well is always preferable to not doing well. So if your kid had the skills to handle disagreements and plans being changed and adults setting limits and demands being placed on him without falling apart, he'd be handling these challenges adaptively. And because he doesn't have the skills, he isn't.

The most important thing you can do to help your explosive kid be less explosive is to understand why he's explosive in the first place. Rule number one: don't place a lot of faith in psychiatric diagnoses. While diagnoses can be helpful in some ways—for example, they "certify" that there's something different about your kid—they don't help you identify the lagging thinking skills underlying your child's explosions; nor do they help you identify the specific problems that are reliably and predictably setting the stage for explosions. Saying that a child has ADHD, or oppositional defiant disorder, or bipolar disorder, or Asperger's disorder, or reactive attachment disorder, or any other disorder, provides no information whatsoever about the thinking skills the child is lacking (and that you could be teaching) or the problems that are precipitating explosions (and that you could be helping him solve).

See, explosive kids don't explode every second of every waking hour. They explode sometimes—with some people, in some situations, on some tasks—in other words, under certain conditions. What are those conditions? Now you know: *whenever he doesn't have the skills to deal well with the demands that are being placed on him.* By the way, that's when all of us are at our worst. The difference between explosive kids and the rest of us is that they fall apart more easily and more often and in more extreme ways than the rest of us do. There's a whole spectrum of maladaptive things kids (and the rest of us) do when life's demands exceed their capacities to respond adaptively. Some kids cry, or pout, or sulk, or withdraw—that's the easy end of the spectrum. Some hold their breath, scream, swear, kick, hit, destroy property, lie, run away, bite, cut themselves, vomit, use weapons, have panic attacks, or worse. This end of the spectrum is of much more concern (and often more dangerous) and requires a more specialized approach.

So you have some hard work ahead of you. Though you probably feel like you're working hard already, the goal is to make sure you have something to show for that hard work. You've already read about the first and most important step in achieving this goal: understanding that if your kid *could* be more flexible, handle frustration more adaptively, and solve problems more proficiently, he would. The next step—also quite important—is to identify the specific lagging skills and unsolved problems that are setting the stage for explosions in your kid. Identifying lagging skills will help you understand *why* your child is exploding. Identifying unsolved problems will help you pinpoint the specific problems—the *who, what, where,* and *when* of explosions—that need to be resolved. Once these problems are solved, your child won't explode over them anymore.

Who's on the hook for identifying the lagging skills and unsolved problems that are coming into play for your kid? You. Your child may well have some very useful information to offer, but extracting that information will depend a great deal on what questions you're asking. You'll probably want to stay away from the following:

Parent: We've talked about this a million times . . . Why don't you just do what you're told? What's the matter with you?
Explosive child: I don't know.

The child's response usually has the effect of further heightening his parents' frustration, but the fact is, the kid is probably telling the truth.

In a perfect world, the child would respond with something like, "See, Mom and Dad, I have a little problem. Actually, it's turning into a big problem. I'm not very good at being flexible, handling frustration, and solving problems. And you guys—and lots of other people—expect me to handle changes in plans, being told what to do, and things not going the way I thought they would as well as other kids. When you expect these things, I start to get frustrated, and then I have trouble thinking clearly, and then I get even more frustrated. Then you guys get frustrated, and that just makes it worse. Then I start doing things I wish I didn't do and saying things I wish I didn't say. Then you sometimes do things you wish you didn't do and say things you wish you didn't say. Then you punish me, and it gets really messy. After the dust settles—you know, when I start thinking clearly again—I end up being really sorry for the things I did and said. I know this isn't fun for you, but rest assured, I'm not having any fun either. I wish we could figure out why I act like this, and work together so it doesn't happen anymore."

Alas, we live in an imperfect world. Explosive kids are rarely able to describe their difficulties with this kind of clarity. But most can provide you with information that will allow for the collaborative method of resolving problems that I describe a little later in this book.

You've just been given a lot of new ideas to digest. Here's a quick summary of the main points:

- Flexibility, frustration tolerance, and problem solving are critical developmental skills that some children fail to learn at an age-appropriate pace. Inadequate development of these skills can contribute to a variety of behaviors—outbursts, explosions, and physical and verbal aggression, often in response to what might seem the most benign or trivial of circumstances—that have a traumatic, adverse impact on these children's interactions and relationships with parents, teachers, siblings, and peers.

- How you explain and understand your child's explosive behavior and the language you use to describe it will directly influence the strategies you use to help your child change this behavior.

- Putting conventional explanations on the shelf will also mean putting conventional parenting practices on the shelf. You need a new plan. But first you've got some figuring out to do.

3

Lagging Skills and
Unsolved Problems

In the last chapter, you read
that lagging skills are *why* kids explode more easily, more
often, and in more extreme ways than the rest of us do;
that unsolved problems are the *who, what, where,* and
when of explosions; that doing well is always preferable
to not doing well (assuming that a kid has the skills to do
well in the first place); and that explosive outbursts occur
when the demands being placed on a child exceed his
capacity to respond adaptively. In this chapter, we move
beyond the general skills of flexibility, frustration tolerance, and problem solving, and consider some of the

more specific lagging skills that set the stage for kids to explode in response to life's challenges.

Now, some folks find the material in this chapter to be rather illuminating; others, despite my best efforts to make things as fascinating as possible, find the content to be, shall we say, less than electrifying. But we're going to plunge ahead, safe in the belief that—you read this in the last chapter, too—*understanding what's getting in the way of explosive kids is the most important part of helping them.* When adults understand how lagging skills can set the stage for explosive outbursts, they take the behavior less personally, respond with greater compassion, and begin to recognize why what they've been thinking and doing about the explosions may have been making things worse.

We're going to sample some lagging skills first and then turn our attention to unsolved problems.

LAGGING SKILLS

> • Difficulty handling transitions, shifting from one mind-set or task to another

This lagging skill contributes to a lot of explosions. Moving from one environment (such as playing outside) to a completely different environment (such as doing homework inside) requires a shift from one mind-set ("When I'm playing outside, it's okay to run around and make noise and socialize") to another ("When I'm doing homework, I need to sit at my desk and concentrate on my schoolwork"). If a kid has difficulty with this skill, there's a good chance he'll be thinking and acting like he's still playing outside long after it's time to settle down for homework. And the situation can grow more precarious when someone is *demanding* that a kid shift rapidly. This would explain why a kid who lacks this skill would run into trouble when, for example, his mother insists that he stop watching television or playing a computer game *immediately* and come into the kitchen for dinner.

That's right, simply telling a kid what to do qualifies as a demand for a shift in mind-set. Interestingly, it's when kids are in the midst of having difficulty shifting that many adults insist even more firmly on instantaneous shifting. Ratcheting things up in this manner greatly diminishes the likelihood of efficient shifting, while also heightening the likelihood of an explosion.

How do we know a child is having difficulty shifting gears? He tells us! Let's listen in:

Parent: I'm running a little behind today. Finish your breakfast, put your dishes in the sink, and get ready for school.

Child: I'm not through eating yet.

Parent: Why don't you grab an apple or something? Come on, hurry! I have to drop some things at the post office on the way there.

Child: I can't do that!

Parent: You can't do what? Why do you always do

this when I'm in a hurry? Just this once, could you please do what I say without giving me a hard time?

Child: I don't know what to do!

Parent: I just told you what to do! Don't push me today!

[kaboom]

Does the fact that your kid has difficulty shifting gears mean you shouldn't tell him what to do anymore? No, but it should help you understand that he's not intentionally trying to be noncompliant, and is instead having trouble flexibly and efficiently shifting from one mind-set to another. Can explosive kids be helped to shift more efficiently? Absolutely. But threats and punishments don't teach this skill.

- Difficulty reflecting on multiple thoughts or ideas simultaneously (disorganized)

- Difficulty considering a range of solutions to a problem

- Difficulty considering the likely outcomes or consequences of actions (impulsive)

Here are three skills that often cluster together, especially when a person is faced with a problem or frustration. What's the main thing your brain must do when faced with a frustration? Solve the problem that's frustrating you. Most of us have never given much thought to the actual thinking processes that are involved in solving a problem, but if you have an explosive kid, it may be worth thinking about. The process involves first identifying the problem you're trying to solve (it's very hard to solve a problem if you don't know what the problem is), then considering the range of options that would help you solve the problem, and then considering the likely outcomes of each potential solution so as to pick the best one.

Many kids are so disorganized in their thinking that they're unable to figure out what problem they're trying to solve. These kids also have difficulty thinking of more than one solution to a problem. And many are so impulsive that even if they could think of more than one solution, they've already done the first thing that popped into their heads. The bad news? The first solution is often the worst one, which explains why such kids are notorious for putting their "worst foot" forward. Problems that don't get solved have a way of sticking around. That's when they qualify as unsolved problems and make explosions even more likely.

By the way, many of these disorganized, impulsive kids evidence a pattern called *reflexive negativity*. This refers to the tendency for them to instantaneously say "No!" every time there's a change in plan or whenever a new idea or request is presented.

Can explosive children be helped to approach problems in a more organized, less impulsive manner so they explode less often? Yes. But sticker charts and time-outs won't teach these skills.

• Difficulty expressing concerns, needs, or thoughts in words

---

Communication skills are absolutely crucial for tolerating frustration, solving problems, and dealing with life's challenges in a flexible, adaptable manner. Navigating life's challenges is far more difficult and frustrating if a kid doesn't have the wherewithal to communicate what's bugging him, what he needs, or what he's thinking. A lot of explosions are set in motion by the lack of these skills.

Many explosive children don't have a basic vocabulary for letting people know they "need a break," that "something's the matter," that they "can't talk about that right now," that they "need a minute" to collect their thoughts or shift gears, or that they "don't like that." Under such circumstances, there's a reasonable chance that alternative verbalizations will be uttered instead: "Screw you," "I hate you," "Shut-up," and "Leave me alone" are some of the milder possibilities. Adults and peers don't tend to take kindly to these alternative expressions, but their reactions don't make it any easier for explosive kids to use more desirable words.

One of the most crucial uses of words is in the solving of problems. Most of the thinking and sorting through we do in solving problems is done in words. And we humans rely almost exclusively on past experience to help us solve similar problems in the present, and those solutions are typically stored as words in our brains. The process of thinking about problems and accessing previous solutions is much more automatic and efficient for children who have intact language processing and communication skills than it is for kids who don't.

Take George, for example:

Therapist: George, I understand you got pretty frustrated at soccer the other day.

George: Yup.

Therapist: What happened?

George: The coach took me out of the game, and I didn't want to come out.

Therapist: So that made you pretty mad, yes?

George: Yup.

Therapist: So what did you do?

George: He wouldn't put me back in, so I kicked him.

Therapist: You kicked the coach?

George: Yup.

Therapist: What happened next?

George: He kicked me off the team.

Therapist: I'm sorry to hear that.

George: I didn't even kick him that hard.

Therapist: I guess it wasn't important how hard you kicked him. I'm just wondering if you can think of something else you could have done when you were mad besides kick the coach.

George: Well, I didn't think of anything else then.

Therapist: Can you think of anything else now?

George: Um . . . I could have asked him when he was going to put me back in.

Therapist: How come you didn't do that instead?

George: I didn't know what to say.

Can children such as George be helped to "use their words" to let us know what's bugging them, what they need, and what they're thinking? To sort through problems and access solutions more efficiently? Yes, of course. But a reward and punishment program won't teach these skills.

> • Difficulty managing emotional response to frustration in order to think rationally
>
> • Chronic irritability and/or anxiety significantly impede capacity for problem solving

Thinking clearly and solving problems are much easier if a person has the capacity to separate or detach himself from the emotions caused by frustration. While emotions can be useful for mobilizing or energizing people to solve a problem, *thinking* is how problems get solved. Once mobilized, the trick is to put one's emotions "on the shelf" in order to think through solutions to problems more objectively, rationally, and logically. Kids who are pretty good at this skill tend to respond to problems or frustrations with more thought than emotion, and that's good. But children whose skills in this domain are lacking tend to respond to problems or frustrations with less thought and more emotion, and that's not good at all. They may actually feel themselves "heating up" but often aren't able to stem the emotional tide until later, when the emotions have subsided and rational thought has kicked back in. They may even have the knowledge to deal successfully with problems and can actually demonstrate such knowledge under calmer circumstances, but at the moment they're frustrated their powerful emotions prevent them from accessing and using the information.

Such kids are not intentionally trying to be noncompliant; rather, they become overwhelmed by the emotions associated with frustration and have difficulty applying rational thought until they calm down. The fact that you're reading this book suggests that you know what this is like:

Parent: It's time to stop playing Nintendo and get ready for bed.

Child, responding with more emotion than thought: Damn! I'm right in the middle of an important game!

Parent, perhaps also responding with more emotion than thought: You're always right in the middle of an important game. Get to bed! Now!

Child: Sh-t! You made me mess up my game!

Parent: I messed up your game? Get your butt in gear before I mess up something else!

[kaboom]

As this dialogue suggests, if you respond to a child who reacts to problems with more emotion than thought by imposing your will more intensively and "teaching him who's the boss," you probably won't help him learn to manage his emotions. Quite the opposite, in fact.

Thinking rationally in the midst of frustration requires immediate, in-the-moment emotion regulation skills. But there are some kids whose difficulties in regulating emotions are more chronic. In other words, there are kids who are irritable, agitated, cranky, and fatigued much more often and much more intensely than others are. Most of us don't handle frustration and solve problems very well when we're in a bad mood. These kids are in a bad mood a lot, so their ability to handle frustration and solve problems is compromised much more.

Are these children depressed? Perhaps, but irritable, cranky, grouchy, or grumpy would probably be more descriptive. Do these children have bipolar disorder? During the past decade, some mental health professionals have developed a troubling tendency to equate "explosive" and "bipolar," to interpret irritability and explosiveness as purely biological phenomena, and to conclude that a poor response to stimulant medications or antidepressants is ample evidence for diagnosing an explosive child as bipolar. This trend probably explains both the astounding rates at which bipolar disorder is being diagnosed in children and the popularity of mood-stabilizing and atypical antipsychotic medications. As you now know, there are many lagging skills that could set the stage for a child to be explosive. And there are many factors that could set the stage for a child to be irritable; brain chemistry is only one. Some children are irritable because of chronic unsolved problems, such as school failure, having no friends, or being bullied. Medicine doesn't fix school failure, having no friends, or being bullied. While there are kids for whom medicine is an indispensable component of treatment, there are many "bipolar" children—*most*, in my experience—whose explosiveness is far better explained by lagging skills and unsolved problems and whose difficulties are therefore not well addressed by the multiple mood-stabilizing medications they have been prescribed. If the only time a child looks like he has bipolar disorder is when he's frustrated, that's not bipolar disorder; that's a developmental delay in the domains of flexibility, frustration tolerance, and problem solving.

What's crystal clear is that the explosiveness of many children is being fueled by a fairly chronic state of irritability and agitation that makes it hard for them to respond to life's routine frustrations in an adaptive, rational manner.

Mother: Mickey, why so grumpy? It's a beautiful day outside. Why are you indoors?

Mickey, slumped in a chair, agitated: It's windy.

Mother: It's windy?

Mickey, more agitated: I said it's windy! I hate wind!

Mother: Mickey, you could be out playing
   basketball, swimming . . . you're this upset over a
   little wind?
Mickey, very agitated: It's too windy, damn it! Leave
   me alone!

Like irritability, anxiety has the potential to make rational thought much more difficult. When a kid is anxious about something—a monster under the bed, an upcoming test, a new or unpredictable situation—clear thinking is essential. But for some kids, clear thinking doesn't take place. The combination of anxiety and irrationality causes some children (the lucky ones) to cry. But it causes others (the unlucky ones) to explode. The criers are the lucky ones because crying is at the milder end of the spectrum, and adults tend to take things far less personally and respond far more empathically to children who cry than to children who explode, even though the two behaviors emanate from the same source: lagging skills and unsolved problems.

Let's use your author as an example. I used to be flight-anxious . . . that's right, scared of flying. The sweaty palms, racing heart, and catastrophic thoughts weren't an intentional bid to get flight attendants to pay attention to me. I was truly unnerved to find myself five miles above the earth going more than five hundred miles per hour in an aluminum apparatus filled with gasoline, with my life in the hands of people (the pilots and air traffic controllers) I'd never met. To control this anxiety, I would engage in a few important rituals to ensure the safe progress of my flight: I had to sit in a window seat so I could scan the skies for threatening aircraft and had to review the emergency instruction card before the plane took off. I knew these rituals worked because all the flights I'd been on had delivered me safely to my destination.

Did these rituals cause me to behave oddly at times? You make the call. On one flight, my plane was cruising along at thirty-three thousand feet or so, and I was, as usual, vigilantly scanning the horizon for foreboding aircraft. Then the unthinkable happened: I spotted an aircraft far off on the horizon ascending in the general direction of my airplane. By my expert calculation, we had about five minutes before the paths of the two planes crossed and my life would come to an abrupt, fiery end. So I did what any very anxious, increasingly irrational, human being would do: I rang for the flight attendant. There was no time to spare.

"Do you see that airplane down there?" I sputtered, pointing toward the speck many miles off in the distance. She peered out the window. "Do you think the captain knows it's there?" I demanded.

The flight attendant tried to hide her amusement (or amazement, I wasn't sure which) and said, "I'll be sure to let him know."

I was greatly relieved, even though I was certain that my heroism was not fully appreciated by either the flight attendant or the passengers seated near me, who were now scanning the aircraft for empty seats to which they could move. Later, the plane landed safely, of course, and as I was leaving the airplane, the flight attendant and pilot were waiting at the door and smiled as I approached. The flight attendant tugged on the pilot's sleeve and introduced me: "Captain, this is the gentleman who was helping you fly the plane."

I'm proud to say that while I still generally prefer window seats, I no longer scan the skies for oncoming aircraft or review the emergency manual (and have survived hundreds of flights on which I did neither). How did I get over my flight anxiety? Experience. And thinking clearly. An Air Florida pilot got the process going (this was obviously a very long time ago, as that particular airline no longer exists). As I was boarding an Air Florida flight, the captain greeted me at the door of the aircraft. I seized the opportunity.

"You're going to fly the plane safely, aren't you?" I implored.

The pilot's response was more helpful than he knew: "What, you think I want to die, buddy?"

That the pilot wasn't particularly enthusiastic about dying was an important revelation, and it got me thinking: about the thousands of planes in the air across the world at any given time and the slim odds of something disastrous happening to the plane that I was on; about the millions of flights that arrive at their destinations uneventfully each year; about the thousands of flights I have been on that arrived safely; about how calm the flight attendants look (except when the plane is struck by lightning, which has now happened to me on two occasions); about how many of my fellow passengers are fast asleep, even when there's turbulence. Quite unintentionally, that Air Florida pilot gave me a new way of thinking that was helpful to me during moments when I was inclined to become highly irrational. Instead of staring out the window, thinking, "What if the wing falls off?" I could instead think a less anxiety-provoking thought such as, "The pilot doesn't want to die" or "The likelihood of something catastrophic happening to my aircraft is really quite slim." The key to helping explosive kids is no different: we need to help them think more rationally. Of course, this often means that we adults need to start thinking more rationally first.

Can irritable or anxious children be helped to regulate their emotions more effectively, to think clearly about problems they're facing? Certainly. But finding new and creative ways to punish them won't teach these skills.

- Difficulty seeing the "grays"; concrete, literal, black-and-white thinking

- Difficulty deviating from rules or routine

- Difficulty handling unpredictability, ambiguity, uncertainty, or novelty

- Difficulty shifting from original idea or solution

- Difficulty taking into account situational factors that would suggest the need to adjust a plan

Very young children tend to be fairly rigid, black-and-white, literal thinkers. That's because they're still making sense of the world, and it's easier to put two and two together if you don't have to worry about exceptions to the rule or alternative ways of looking at things. As children develop, they learn that, in fact, most things in life are "gray"; there *are* exceptions to the rules and alternative ways of interpreting things. We don't go home from grandma's house the same way every time; we don't eat dinner at the exact same time every day; and the weather doesn't always cooperate with our plans. Unfortunately, for some children, "gray" thinking doesn't develop readily. Though some are diagnosed with autism spectrum disorders, these children are better thought of as *black-and-white thinkers living in a gray world*. They often have significant difficulty approaching the world in a flexible, adaptable way and become extremely frustrated when events don't proceed in the manner they had originally configured.

More specifically, these children often have a strong preference for predictability and routines, and struggle when events are unpredictable, uncertain, and ambiguous. These are the kids who run into trouble when they need to adjust or reconfigure their expectations, who tend to overfocus on facts and details, and who often have trouble recognizing the obvious or "seeing the big picture." For example, a child may insist on going out for recess at a certain time on a given day because it is the time the class always goes out for recess, failing to take into account both the likely consequences of insisting on the original plan of action (being at recess alone) and important situational factors (an assembly, perhaps) that would suggest the need for an adaptation in plan. These children may experience enormous frustration as they struggle to apply concrete rules to a world where few such rules apply:

Child, in a car: Dad, this isn't the way we usually go home.
Father, driving: I thought we'd go a different way this time, just for a change of pace.
Child: But this isn't the right way!
Father: I know this isn't the way we usually go, but it may be even faster.
Child: We can't go this way! It's not the same! I don't know this way!
Father: Look, it's not that big a deal to go a different way every once in a while.
[kaboom]

Jennifer (star of the waffle episode in chapter 1) was a black-and-white thinker living in a gray world. So are lots of other explosive kids. Can they be helped to think in a more flexible manner? You bet. But not if the adults around them are being inflexible themselves.

That overview of lagging skills wasn't so bad, was it? Of course, that was just a sampling of the lagging skills that can set the stage for explosions. Here's the complete list, including those we just reviewed:

____ Difficulty handling transitions, shifting from one mind-set or task to another

____ Difficulty doing things in a logical sequence or prescribed order

____ Difficulty mustering the mental energy to persist on challenging or tedious tasks

____ Poor sense of time

____ Difficulty reflecting on multiple thoughts or ideas simultaneously

____ Difficulty maintaining focus for goal-directed problem solving

____ Difficulty considering the likely outcomes or consequences of actions (impulsiveness)

____ Difficulty considering a range of solutions to a problem

____ Difficulty expressing concerns, needs, or thoughts in words

____ Difficulty understanding what is being said

____ Difficulty managing emotional response to frustration in order to think rationally

____ Chronic irritability or anxiety that significantly impedes the capacity for problem solving

____ Difficulty seeing the "grays"; concrete, literal, black-and-white thinking

____ Difficulty deviating from rules or routine

____ Difficulty handling unpredictability, ambiguity, uncertainty, novelty

_____ Difficulty shifting from original idea or solution

_____ Difficulty taking into account situational factors that would suggest the need to adjust a plan

_____ Inflexible, inaccurate interpretations; cognitive distortions or biases (e.g., "Everyone's out to get me," "Nobody likes me," "You always blame me, "It's not fair," "I'm stupid," "Things will never work out for me")

_____ Difficulty attending to or accurately interpreting social cues; poor perception of social nuances

_____ Difficulty starting conversations, entering groups, connecting with people; lack of basic social skills

_____ Difficulty seeking attention in appropriate ways

_____ Difficulty appreciating how one's behavior affects other people; surprise at others' responses

_____ Difficulty empathizing with others and appreciating another person's perspective or point of view

_____ Difficulty appreciating how s/he is coming across or being perceived by others

If after reading this list you've concluded that your explosive child has quite a few lagging skills, then you may be feeling a little overwhelmed at the moment. While there is definitely some hard work in your future, it probably isn't going to be as daunting as it may seem. For now, the most important thing to recognize is that these skills do not come naturally to all children. We tend to think that all children are created equal in these capacities, and this assumption causes many adults to believe that explosive children must not *want* to do well.

As you now know, this simply isn't true. Remember, a kid will always prefer adaptive behavior to maladaptive behavior if he has the skills to pull it off.

By the way, there's a big difference between interpreting lagging skills as *excuses* rather than as *explanations*. When lagging skills are invoked as excuses, the door slams shut on the process of thinking about how to help a child. Conversely, when lagging skills are used as explanations for a child's behavior, the door to helping the child swings wide open, for adults have been provided with an improved understanding of what's getting in the child's way.

Before we turn our attention to unsolved problems, I should mention that your new awareness of the true factors that set the stage for explosive behavior means that some of the terminology you and a lot of others may have been using to "explain" your child's explosions won't make much sense anymore.

- *He just wants attention.*

     This common cliché is often invoked to explain why kids explode . . . but since we *all* want attention, it doesn't help us understand what's really getting in the kid's way, and it doesn't answer the more critical questions: If the kid has the skills to seek attention adaptively, then why is he seeking attention in such a maladaptive fashion? Doesn't the fact that he's seeking attention maladaptively tell us he doesn't have the skills to seek attention adaptively?

- *He just wants his own way.*

  We all want our own way, so this cliché doesn't add any new information, either. Nor does it help us understand why this kid is going about getting his own way in such a maladaptive fashion. Adaptively getting one's own way requires a lot of skills often found lacking in explosive kids.

- *He's manipulating us.*

  Here we have another popular but inaccurate and misguided way of portraying explosive kids. Competent manipulation requires various skills—forethought, planning, impulse control, organization—that are typically found lacking in explosive kids.

- *He's not motivated.*

  If it's true that *kids do well if they can*, then the kid is already motivated and needs something else from us besides rewards and punishment. Remember, if the kid *could* do well, he *would* do well, so poor motivation is unlikely to be what is truly keeping him from doing well. Rewards and punishment don't teach lagging thinking skills and don't solve the problems that precipitate explosive outbursts.

- *He's making bad choices.*

  This suggests that the kid already has the skills to be making good choices. Of course, if he had those skills, we wouldn't be wondering why he's making so many bad choices!

- *He has a bad attitude.*

  He probably didn't start out with one. "Bad attitudes" tend to be the by-product of countless years of being misunderstood and overpunished by adults who didn't recognize that a kid lacked crucial thinking skills. But kids are resilient; they come around if we start doing the right thing.

- *He knows just what buttons to push.*

  We should paraphrase this one so it's more accurate: *when he's having difficulty being flexible, dealing adaptively with frustration, and solving problems, he does things that are very maladaptive and that I experience as being extremely unpleasant.* Good, we agree.

- *He has a mental illness.*

  I'm not sure what this means anymore. If it simply means that a kid qualifies for a psychiatric diagnosis, then, at the risk of redundancy, I should point out that we still don't know what skills he's lacking or what unsolved problems are reliably and predictably precipitating his explosive outbursts. I prefer the term *problems in living* to the term *mental illness*, for it points us in the direction of what really needs to be done for us to help explosive kids: solve the problems that are setting the stage for their explosions.

UNSOLVED PROBLEMS

So now let's turn our attention to the *who, what, where,* and *when* of explosive outbursts. Don't let the fact that this section is at the end of the chapter fool you; in reducing explosive outbursts, unsolved problems are every bit as important as lagging skills.

An unsolved problem is any trigger, situation, circumstance, or condition that reliably and predictably precipitates explosive episodes. An explosive kid doesn't explode every second of every waking hour . . . he explodes *sometimes*: in certain places (where), with certain people (who), during certain times of the day (when), over certain tasks or issues (what). Most explosive kids are set off by the same five or six unsolved problems every day or every week. Why are they called *unsolved problems*? Because if they were already solved, they wouldn't continue to precipitate explosive outbursts.

Need some examples? Let's start with homework, which seems to be the number one problem that triggers explosions in North American households. If homework reliably and predictably precipitates explosions, then homework is a problem that has yet to be solved. If disagreements over the amount of time your kid should spend in front of the TV or computer screen cause explosions, then screen time is an unsolved problem. Here's a list that might be helpful, though it's not exhaustive, so feel free to add your own:

Home
_____ Waking up or getting out of bed in the morning
_____ Completing morning routine or getting ready for school
_____ Sensory hypersensitivities (e.g., the "feel" of clothing)
_____ Starting or completing homework
_____ Food quantities, choices, preferences, or meal timing
_____ Time spent in front of a screen (TV, video games, computer) and choices of games and programming
_____ Going to or getting ready for bed at night
_____ Boredom
_____ Sibling interactions
_____ Cleaning room
_____ Completing household chores or responsibilities
_____ Taking medicine
_____ Riding in car or wearing seatbelt

School
_____ Shifting from one specific task to another
_____ Getting started on or completing class assignments
_____ Interactions with a particular classmate or teacher
_____ Being in the hallway, at recess, in the cafeteria, on the school bus, or waiting in line
_____ Talking at inappropriate times

_____ Specific academic tasks or demands (e.g., writing)
_____ Handling disappointment, losing at a game, not coming in first, or not being first in line

Ready for some homework? I hope so, because reducing explosions isn't going to happen if you don't enact what you're reading in this book. Here's your assignment: make a list of your kid's lagging skills and unsolved problems. The lagging skills help you understand why your kid is explosive. The unsolved problems help you understand with whom, over what, where, and when your kid explodes. As I indicated, the above list of unsolved problems isn't exhaustive—make sure yours includes all the situations that cause disagreements and conflict between you and your child.

Once you figure out what skills your kid is lacking and identify the unsolved problems that are precipitating explosions, the explosions become *highly predictable*. Lots of folks believe that explosions are unpredictable and occur "out of the blue." That's why they wait until a problem shows up (again) before they try to deal with it. That's seldom an effective or reliable strategy. Luckily, because explosions are highly predictable—they occur whenever a kid doesn't have the skills to deal with demands that are being placed on him and when specific unsolved problems show up (again)—they can be prevented *proactively*. Once the problems are solved and the skills are taught, it's hard to imagine why your kid would still be exploding.

There's one more mantra to think about as we near the end of this chapter. It's the definition of good parenting:

Good parenting means being responsive to the hand you've been dealt.

Now that you have a better sense of the hand you've been dealt, most of the rest of the book is aimed at helping you be more responsive to that hand.

YOU

Now, why would a chapter describing lagging skills and unsolved problems and how they set the stage for explosions end with *you*? Well, if explosions occur when the demands and expectations being placed on a kid exceed his capacity to respond adaptively, then the kid is only half of the equation. So it would probably make sense to consider the other half: what expectations you're placing on your kid, whether those expectations are truly realistic, and, especially, how you're going about getting your expectations met. How you go about handling unmet expectations makes all the difference in the world. Thus, as you continue reading, *you* are going to be to an increasingly important part of the picture. Explosions don't occur in a vacuum. It takes two to tango.

Here are the important points of this chapter:

- There are various lagging skills that can make it difficult for a kid to respond to life's challenges in an adaptive, rational manner.

- One of the biggest favors you can do for an explosive kid is to identify the lagging skills that are setting the stage for his challenging behavior so that you and others understand what's getting in his way.

- The other big favor you can do for an explosive kid is to identify the specific unsolved problems that are reliably and predictably precipitating his explosive episodes.

- A form listing all of the lagging skills and unsolved problems described in this chapter can be downloaded at www.explosivechild.com.

- We're going to significantly reduce explosions in your household by changing the way you go about trying to solve those problems with your kid. As you shall see.

4

Drama in Real Life

I'd like to introduce you to some explosive kids—kids who have many redeeming qualities but who become frustrated far more easily and often than other kids and, when they are beyond the brink, do things that are far more extreme. Each has a unique mix of lagging skills and unsolved problems that set the stage for their explosions. Each has parents struggling to figure out what is going on and trying to find a way to handle their kids' explosions in a way that works better than what they're doing now. There's a good chance you'll see similarities between the kids and parents who are described in this chapter (and revisited in one way or another throughout the book) and you and your own kids.

CASEY

Casey is a six-year-old boy living with his parents and younger sister. His parents describe Casey as very hyperactive and irritable and report that he has difficulty playing by himself and isn't great at playing with other kids, either. They indicate that Casey seems to be quite bright, in that he has excellent memory for factual information, but that he becomes anxious when presented with new tasks or situations. They also report that Casey is quite limited in the clothes he'll wear and the food he's willing to eat. He often complains that certain fabrics and labels are annoying to him and that many common foods "smell funny." And his parents say that he has a lot of trouble with transitions. Getting him to come indoors after playing outside is often a major ordeal.

Casey's parents have read a lot about ADHD and think that this diagnosis fits their son, but they also realize that many of his difficulties fall outside the realm of this disorder. Having read books on bipolar disorder as well, they wonder if Casey's explosions and irritability mean he's bipolar, but they aren't sure he's "manic" or "grandiose" enough to qualify. They feel the term *control freak* fits their son better than any traditional diagnosis.

Casey's explosions at home usually consist of screaming, crying, and occasionally hitting. The parents often try to talk to Casey about these behaviors, but even when he's in a good mood, his capacity for thinking and talking about his behavior seems limited; after a few seconds, he yells, "I can't talk about this right now!" and ends the conversation, often by running out of the room.

His parents previously consulted a psychologist, who helped them establish a point system through which Casey was rewarded for good behavior and punished for behaviors that were less desirable. They vigilantly implemented the program but found that Casey's hyperactivity, inflexibility, and irritability overpowered his clear desire to obtain rewards and avoid punishments. The program actually seemed to frustrate Casey further, but the psychologist encouraged his parents to stick with it, certain that Casey's behavior would improve. It didn't, so they discontinued the program after about three months.

"We need something else," his mother pleads. "He's destroying our family."

Casey has difficulties at school, too. Like his parents, Casey's first-grade teacher is impressed by his factual knowledge but concerned by his poor problem-solving skills. When lessons involve recall of rote information, Casey is the star of the class. When lessons require the application of this information to more abstract, complex, real-life situations, his responses are disorganized and off the mark. When he is frustrated by a particular task, he often yells, "I can't do this!" and becomes agitated or starts crying; sometimes he runs out of the classroom. On several occasions, he has run out of the school, which caused great concern for his safety. Sometimes he regains his composure quickly; other times it takes twenty to thirty minutes for him to calm down. Afterward, Casey is either remorseful ("I'm sorry I ran out of the classroom . . . I know I shouldn't do that") or has difficulty remembering the episode.

Casey's teacher reports that she can often tell from the moment Casey walks through the door in the morning that he is going to have a tough day. But she also observes that Casey is capable of falling apart even when his day seems to be going smoothly. The teacher is becoming increasingly concerned about Casey's relationships with other children. She reports that Casey occasionally hits or yells at other children during less structured activities, particularly when he does not get his way. Casey seems to lack an appreciation for the impact of his actions on others and seems unable to use the feedback he receives from others to adjust his behavior.

That's a lot to digest! Let's see if we can make the above information more manageable by viewing it through the prism of lagging skills and unsolved problems. We'll start with lagging skills, in other words, *why* Casey is having so much difficulty:

- Difficulty handling transitions, shifting from one mind-set or task to another

- Difficulty considering a range of solutions to a problem

- Difficulty managing emotional response to frustration in order to think rationally

- Chronic irritability or anxiety that significantly impedes the capacity for problem solving

- Difficulty seeing the "grays"; concrete, literal, black-and-white thinking

- Difficulty appreciating how his behavior is affecting other people

Next, let's identify the problems that need to be solved, the *who, what, where,* and *when* of Casey's explosions. Once these problems are solved, Casey won't be exploding over them anymore. Notice that this isn't a list of what Casey *does* when he's upset but rather what problems are *causing* him to get upset in the first place:

- Playing by himself

- Playing with other kids

- Doing something new or unfamiliar

- Wearing certain clothes

- Eating certain foods

- Coming indoors after playing outside

- Talking about his problems

These problems won't be solved in one fell swoop; they'll be solved systematically, one at a time. And, in solving these problems—collaboratively—Casey and his parents will learn some new skills, eliminate some very counterproductive interactions, and reduce the likelihood of explosions.

HELEN

Helen is an eight-year-old girl whose parents describe her as charming, sensitive, creative, energetic, and sociable. But they also describe her as intense, easily angered, argumentative, resistant, and "impossible to reason with" when she's frustrated. They report that Helen tends to fall apart when things don't go exactly as she anticipates or when she's presented with new things. For example, Helen had a full-blown, four-hour explosion because she couldn't get her hair to look the way she wanted it to. And her teacher reports that Helen—who is not explosive at school—does balk when presented with new or unfamiliar assignments. Her parents say that weekends are especially difficult; although Helen doesn't love going to school, she becomes bored during unstructured weekend time and is difficult to please. Psychoeducational testing indicates that while Helen is above average in intelligence, she has difficulty communicating her thoughts in spoken language.

In one of their early meetings with Helen's therapist,

her parents recounted one of her explosions during the previous week.

"On Tuesday, Helen told me she'd like to have chili for dinner the next night," recalled her father. "So, on Wednesday afternoon, I left work a little early and made her the chili she had asked for. When she got home from swimming late Wednesday afternoon, she seemed a little tired; when I announced to her that I had made her the chili she wanted, she grumbled, 'I want macaroni and cheese.' This took me a little bit by surprise, since I know she really loves chili. It was also a little irritating, since I had put time into doing something nice for her. So I told her she would have to eat the chili. But she seemed unable to get macaroni and cheese out of her head, and I continued to insist that she eat the chili for dinner. The more I insisted, the more she fell apart. Eventually, she lost it completely. She was screaming and crying, but I was determined that she would eat the chili I had made her."

"What did you do then?" the therapist asked.

"We sent her to her bedroom and told her she had to stay there until she was ready to eat the chili," said Helen's mother. "For the next hour she screamed and cried in her room; at one point, she was banging on her mirror and broke it. Can you imagine? All this over chili! I went up to her room a few times to see if I could calm her down, but it was impossible. Helen was totally irrational. The amazing thing is that, at one point, she couldn't even remember what she was upset about."

"Why was it so important to you that she eat the chili instead of the macaroni and cheese?" the therapist asked.

"Because I inconvenienced myself to do something nice for her," the father responded.

"Sounds like a legitimate concern to me," the therapist said. "Do you think that your enduring this explosion—having Helen go nuts in her room for an hour, breaking her mirror, and ruining your evening—made it any less likely that she'll explode the next time she's frustrated over something similar?"

"No," the parents responded instantaneously.

"What was Helen like when the episode was all over?" the therapist asked.

"Very remorseful and very loving," the mother responded. "It's hard to know whether to reciprocate her affection or to hold a grudge for a while to cement the point that we don't like that kind of behavior."

"Well," the therapist replied, "if you don't think that inducing and enduring explosions is going to help her deal better with frustration the next time, then it follows that holding a grudge probably isn't going to help either."

"Yes, but how will she learn that that kind of behavior is unacceptable?" asked the mother.

"From what I can gather," the therapist said, "the fact that you disapprove of that kind of behavior is pretty well cemented in her mind already, so I doubt that we'll be needing more cement. She also seems genuinely motivated to please you both and seems as miserable about her explosions as you are. So I doubt that adding additional misery to the mix will help."

What Helen and her parents did need was a different way to resolve disagreements and problems.

What skills was Helen lacking?

- Difficulty expressing concerns, needs, or thoughts in words

- Difficulty managing emotional response to frustration in order to think rationally

- Difficulty deviating from rules, routine, or original plan

- Difficulty handling unpredictability, ambiguity, uncertainty, novelty, or surprises

- Difficulty shifting from original idea or solution

- Difficulty adapting to changes in plan or new rules

- Difficulty taking into account situational factors that would suggest the need to adjust a plan

And unsolved problems? We probably don't have a complete picture yet, but we do know a few:

- Hair not looking the way she wants

- Unstructured time over the weekend

- Being presented with new or unfamiliar assignments at school

DANNY

Danny is a fifth grader whose mother describes him as moody, irritable, and very easily frustrated. She is especially concerned about what she refers to as Danny's "rage attacks," which have occurred numerous times every week since Danny was a toddler. During such episodes, he becomes verbally abusive and physically aggressive. His mother is also worried about how these attacks are affecting Danny's sister, who at times seems scared of her older brother and at other times seems to take pleasure in provoking him. Danny has never had an explosive outburst at school.

Danny's parents divorced amicably when he was seven and still consider themselves "co-parents." He and his younger sister stay with their father and his fiancée every other weekend.

Danny has seen numerous mental health professionals over the years. Like many explosive kids, he has accumulated a fairly impressive number of psychiatric diagnoses, including oppositional-defiant disorder, depression, and bipolar disorder. His family physician medicated Danny with Ritalin several years previous, but Danny remained moody, rigid, and explosive. A psychiatrist had subsequently prescribed an antidepressant, but this medication caused Danny to become significantly more agitated and hyperactive.

"Danny can be in a perfectly pleasant mood and then—bang!—something doesn't go quite the way he thought it would, and he's swearing and hitting," his mother reports.

"I don't know what to do. The other day he and I were in the car together and I took a wrong turn. Danny suddenly became very agitated that we weren't going the right way. All of a sudden, I had a ten-year-old kid punching me! In the car! While I'm driving! It's insanity!

"I'm tired of people telling me this behavior is occurring because I'm a single parent. My ex-husband is still very much involved in Danny's life, and there hasn't been any of the backstabbing that takes place with some divorces. I will say I think his dad tries too hard to be Danny's best friend. But these explosions started way before there were problems in our marriage. I must admit, though, Danny's a lot more explosive when he's with me than he is when he's with his dad."

After Danny explodes, he seems genuinely contrite over the behavior his mother describes. He tells his mom he's trying very hard not to be physically or verbally aggressive but can't seem to control himself in the midst of frustration. He tells his father that he explodes more with his mother because she "nags too much."

In a session with a family therapist with whom they'd begun working, Danny's mother described his biggest explosion of the week. "Yesterday, I told him he had to come in from playing basketball to eat dinner. He whined a little, but I insisted. Next thing I know, his face is red, he's calling me every name in the book, he's accusing me of ruining his life, and I'm hiding behind a door trying to shield myself from getting kicked. I was petrified. So was his sister. And it's not the first time. Twenty minutes later, he was sorry. But this is just ridiculous. I'm sick of being hit, and it's just impossible to reason with him once he gets going."

"What did you do once he'd calmed down?" the family therapist asked.

"I punished him for swearing at me and trying to kick me," replied the mother. "I feel he needs to be disciplined for that kind of behavior."

"I can understand you feeling that way. Tell me, have you always punished him when he's acted like that?"

Danny's mother looked determined. "You bet. I'm not willing to just let that kind of disrespect slide."

"What happens when you punish him?" the family therapist asked.

The look of determination faded. "He goes nuts. It's horrible."

"But despite all the punishing, he's still very verbally and physically aggressive, yes?"

Danny's mother smiled through gritted teeth. "That's why I'm here."

"Well," the family therapist said, "I'm all in favor of punishment when it's productive—you know, when it's effective at changing a child's behavior. But I'm not sure punishment makes sense just for the sake of punishment."

"What, I should let him get away with what he does?" demanded the mother.

"Don't get me wrong," the family therapist said. "We need to help him stop exploding and hitting. But based on what you've been telling me, 'not letting him get away with it' hasn't changed his behavior at all."

Danny's mother pondered this observation for a moment. "I think I figured that eventually the message would get through if I just kept plugging away. I never stopped to think that maybe the message would never get through."

"Oh, I suspect Danny knows you don't like his behavior," the therapist said. "In fact, I'm reasonably certain he even knows how you'd like him to behave instead."

"Then why doesn't he?" the mother demanded.

"Now that I've met with Danny a few times, I get the feeling he's generally in a pretty cranky mood. I know he's not crazy about coming here, but is that his mood most of the time?" the therapist asked.

"Absolutely," replied the mother. "We call him Grumpy. He doesn't seem to enjoy himself very much, and he's very uptight. Everything seems to bother him."

"What an unpleasant existence," the therapist empathized. "And it has very unpleasant implications for everyone around him."

Danny's mother sighed. "You can say that again. But what does that have to do with his being explosive and angry and trying to hurt me?"

"Well, if we view him as grumpy and irritable, rather than as disrespectful and oppositional, then I think our approach to dealing with him might look a lot different," the therapist said.

"I don't understand what you mean," said the mother.

"What I mean is that kids who are grumpy and irritable don't usually need more discipline," the family therapist said. "I've yet to see discipline be especially useful at helping a kid be less irritable and agitated."

So, based on the above information, what do we know about *why* Danny explodes?

- Difficulty considering a range of solutions to a problem

- Difficulty managing emotional response to frustration in order to think rationally

- Chronic irritability or anxiety that significantly impedes the capacity for problem solving

- Difficulty deviating from rules or routine

- Difficulty handling unpredictability, ambiguity, uncertainty, or novelty

- Difficulty shifting from original idea or solution

- Difficulty adapting to changes in plan or new rules

We have some early ideas about the *who, what, where,* and *when* of Danny's explosions, too:

- Being nagged by mother (we'd need to know more about the specific things his mother is nagging him about)

- Coming in from playing outside

MITCHELL

Mitchell is a fifteen-year-old ninth grader whose parents were convinced he needed to see yet another in a long line of therapists. At the first session, the therapist met with Mitchell's parents before seeing Mitchell. His mother, a law professor, and father, a practicing lawyer, told the therapist that Mitchell had been diagnosed with both Tourette's disorder and bipolar disorder but was refusing all medication except an antihypertensive, which he was taking to control his tics. They also said that Mitchell was extremely unhappy about having been brought to the office that day, for he greatly distrusted mental health professionals.

The parents reported that Mitchell—their youngest child (his siblings were already living outside the home)—was extremely irritable, had no friends, and became frustrated at the drop of a hat. They indicated that Mitchell was extremely bright and very eccentric but was repeating the ninth grade because of a rough time he'd had at a local prep school the year before.

"This is a classic case of wasted potential," said the father. "We were devastated by what happened last year."

"What happened?" the therapist asked.

"He just plain bombed out of prep school," said the father. "Here's a kid with an IQ in the 140s, and he's not making it at one of the area's top prep schools. He practically had a nervous breakdown over it. He had to be hospitalized for a week because he tried to slit his wrists."

"That sounds very serious and very scary. How is he now?" the therapist asked.

"Lousy," said the mother. "He has no self-esteem left. He's lost all faith in himself. And he doesn't seem to be able to complete any schoolwork anymore. We think he's depressed."

"Where's he going to school now?" the therapist asked.

"Our local high school," the mother replied. "They're very nice there and everything, but we don't think he's being challenged by the work, bright as he is."

"Of course, there's more to doing well in school besides smarts," the therapist said. "Can I take a look at the testing you had done?"

The parents gave the therapist a copy of a psycho-educational evaluation that had been performed when Mitchell was in the seventh grade. The report documented a twenty-five-point discrepancy between his exceptional verbal skills and average nonverbal skills, difficulty on tasks sensitive to distractibility, very slow processing speed, and below-average written language skills. But, amazingly, the examiner had concluded that Mitchell had no difficulties that would interfere with his learning.

"This is an interesting report," the therapist said.

"How's that?" asked the father.

"Well, it may give us some clues as to why Mitchell might be struggling to live up to everyone's expectations in school," the therapist said.

"We were told he had no learning problems," the mother said.

"I think that was probably inaccurate," the therapist said. He then explained the potential ramifications of some of the evaluation findings. As they talked, it became clear that Mitchell was struggling most on tasks involving a lot of writing, problem solving, rapid processing, and sustained effort. "That's something we're going to have to take a much closer look at," the therapist said.

"Of course, he's still very bright," said the father.

"There are some areas in which he is clearly quite bright," the therapist said. "And some things that may be making it very hard for him to show how bright he is. My bet is that he finds that disparity quite frustrating."

"Oh, he's frustrated, all right," said the mother. "We all are."

After a while, Mitchell was invited to come into the office. He refused to meet with the therapist alone, so his parents remained in the room.

"I'm sick of mental health professionals," Mitchell announced from the outset.

"How come?" the therapist asked.

"Never had much use for them. None of them has ever done me any good," Mitchell answered.

"Don't be rude, Mitchell," his father intoned.

"SHUT UP, FATHER!" Mitchell boomed. "HE WASN'T TALKING TO YOU!"

The storm passed quickly. "It sounds like you've been through quite a bit in the past two years," the therapist said.

"WHAT DID YOU TELL HIM?!" Mitchell boomed at his parents.

"We told him about the trouble you had in prep school," the mother answered, "and about your being suicidal, and about how we don't . . ."

"ENOUGH!" Mitchell screamed. "I don't know this man from Adam, and you've already told him my life story! And I wouldn't have been suicidal if I hadn't been on about eighty-seven different medications at the time!"

"What were you taking back then?" the therapist asked.

"I don't know," Mitchell said, rubbing hard on his forehead. "You tell him, Mother!"

"I think he's been on about every psychiatric drug known to mankind," said the mother. "Lithium, Prozac . . ."

"STOP EXAGGERATING, MOTHER!" Mitchell boomed.

"Mitchell, don't be rude to your mother," said the father.

"If you don't stop telling me not to be rude, I'm leaving!" Mitchell screamed.

Once again, the storm quickly subsided. "What medicines are you taking now?" the therapist asked.

"Just something for my tics," Mitchell replied. "And don't even think about telling me to take something else! Let's just get off this topic!"

"He doesn't even take his tic medication all the time," said the mother. "That's why he still tics so much."

"MOTHER, STOP!" Mitchell boomed. "I don't care about the tics! Leave me alone about them!"

"It's just that . . ." the mother began speaking again.

"MOTHER, NO!" Mitchell boomed. His mother stopped.

"Mitchell, are you suicidal now?" the therapist asked.

"NO! And if you ask me that again, I'm leaving!"

"He still doesn't feel very good about himself, though," the father said.

"I FEEL JUST FINE!" Mitchell boomed. "You're the ones who need a psychologist, not me!" Mitchell turned to the therapist. "Can you do something about them?" The father chuckled at this question.

"WHAT'S SO FUNNY?!" Mitchell boomed.

"If I might interrupt," the therapist said, "I know you didn't want to be here today, and I can understand why you might not have much faith in yet another mental health professional. But I'm interested . . . what is it you'd like me to do about your parents?"

"Tell them to leave me alone," he growled. "I'm fine."

"Yes, he's got everything under complete control," the father said sarcastically.

"PLEASE!" Mitchell boomed.

"If I told them to leave you alone, do you think they would?" the therapist asked.

Mitchell glared at his parents. "No, I don't."

The therapist chose his words carefully. "Is it fair to say that your interactions with your parents are very frustrating for you?"

Mitchell turned to his parents. "You've found another genius," he said. "We need to pay money and waste our time on this guy telling us the obvious?"

"Mitchell!" said the father. "Don't be rude!"

"STOP TELLING ME WHAT TO DO!" Mitchell boomed.

"I appreciate your looking out for me," the therapist said to the father. "But I actually want to hear what Mitchell has to say." The therapist looked back at Mitchell. "I don't think I can get them to leave you alone without your being here."

"I don't think you can get them to leave me alone with me being here," Mitchell said. Then he paused for a moment. "How often do I have to come?" he asked.

"Well, to start, I'd like you to come every other week," the therapist said. "I'd like your parents to come every week. Is that reasonable?"

"Fine!" he said. "Can we leave now?"

You've already been given your first homework assignment (maybe you've even completed it), but are you ready for your first quiz? What skills is Mitchell lacking? And what unsolved problems are reliably and predictably precipitating his explosive outbursts?

At this point you might be thinking, "Wow, I don't have it so bad," or, "Does he think we don't know what explosions look like?" or, "Can we please get on with the show

here? Tell me what to do!" We're getting there, I promise. But we have one more avenue to explore. We need to
think about why the things you've done already to reduce
your child's explosions may not have worked very well
and may even have made things worse.

5

The Truth About Consequences

You know, first we thought Amy was just a willful, stubborn kid," one father recalls. "We had all these books, and TV personalities, and those nanny shows, and our pediatrician telling us that if we were simply firmer and more consistent with her, things would get better. Amy's grandparents added their two cents; they were constantly telling my wife and me about how Amy would have been handled in the 'good old days.' But all that advice didn't help much. Eventually it became obvious that we were going to need professional help.

"The first doctor told us Amy had a lot of anger and rage. Amy spent the next year in play therapy, with this therapist trying to figure out what she was so angry about. He sort of ignored us when we told him Amy wasn't angry all the time, only when things didn't go exactly the way she thought they would. He never did figure out why she was so angry.

"The next doctor said that Amy's tantrums were just her trying to get her way and get us to pay attention to her. He tried to convince us that Amy's explosions are our fault. If it's our fault, how come our other two kids are so well behaved? He told us to ignore the tantrums and give her lots of attention for good behaviors. But ignoring her didn't help her calm down when she was frustrated about something. I don't care what the experts say, you can't just ignore your kid when she's being destructive and violent. This doctor also taught us how to do the whole sticker chart and time-out routine. It makes me shudder to think of how much time that poor kid spent in time-out, and of what my wife and I went through trying to keep her there. But we were told the lessons we were trying to teach her would eventually sink in.

"Eventually, this doctor came to the conclusion that since all those time-outs didn't seem to be doing the trick, Amy needed medication to help her hold it together better. We weren't all that enthusiastic about the idea, but we took Amy to a child psychiatrist anyway. We figured we had nothing to lose. But when the first medicine didn't get the job done, she added another . . . then another. I'm sure there are some kids who do well on meds, but Amy wasn't one of them. All she had to show for all that medication was an extra thirty pounds. In the meantime, we're still trying to figure out how to live with a kid like this.

"We've paid a big price—and I'm not just talking about money—listening to different doctors and doing what they said. We still don't understand why Amy acts the way she does, and we still don't know what to do about it."

Probably the most common approach to understanding and changing the behavior of explosive children derives from the conventional wisdom: somewhere along the line, explosive kids have learned that their tantrums, explosions, swearing, screaming, and destructiveness bring them attention or help them get their way by convincing their parents to "give in." This belief often gives rise to the notion that explosions are planned, intentional, purposeful, and under the child's conscious control ("He's a very manipulative kid. He knows exactly what buttons to push!"), which, in turn, often causes adults to take the behavior very personally ("Why is he doing this to me? I don't deserve this!"). As you read in chapter 2, the corollary to the belief that such behavior is learned is that the child has been poorly taught or disciplined by passive, permissive, inconsistent parents ("What that kid needs is parents who let him know who's the boss and don't back down!"). Parents who become convinced of this often blame themselves for their child's explosive behavior ("We must be doing something wrong . . . nothing we do seems to work with this kid"). Finally, if you believe that such behavior is learned and is the result of poor parenting and lax discipline, then it follows that it can also be unlearned with better and more convincing teaching and discipline.

In general, this unlearning and re-teaching process includes (1) providing the kid with lots of positive attention for good behavior to reduce the likelihood that he will seek attention by exhibiting maladaptive behavior; (2) teaching parents to issue fewer and clearer commands; (3) teaching the kid that compliance is expected and enforced on all parental commands and that he must comply quickly because his parents are going to issue a command only once or twice; (4) teaching the child that his parents won't back down in the face of explosions; (5) maintaining a record-keeping and currency system (points, stickers, checks, happy faces, and the like) to track the child's performance on specified target behaviors, such as complying with adult commands, doing homework, getting ready for school, brushing teeth, and so forth; and (6) delivering consequences—rewards, such as allowance money and special privileges, and punishments, such as time-outs, grounding, and the loss of privileges—contingent on the child's successful or unsuccessful performance. This conventional approach isn't magic; it merely formalizes practices that have long been considered important cornerstones of effective parenting: being clear about how a child should and should not behave, consistently expecting and insisting on appropriate behavior, and giving a child the incentive to perform such behavior.

Some parents and their children benefit from such programs and find that these procedures add some needed structure and organization to family discipline. Other parents may embark on a behavior management program with an initial burst of enthusiasm, energy, and vigilance, but become less enthusiastic, energetic, and vigilant over time and return to their old, familiar patterns of parenting. And many parents find that behavior management procedures don't improve their child's behavior, even when they stick with the program. In fact, some parents find that such programs may actually *increase* the frequency and intensity of their kid's explosions and cause their interactions with their kid to worsen. How can this be? Don't reward and punishment programs work for everyone?

No, they don't. No intervention works for everyone and everything. Antibiotics work for some things and not for others. Aspirin works for some things and wouldn't be the treatment of choice for others. Chemotherapy works for some things and not well at all for others. And reward and punishment programs work for some things and not for others.

Reward and punishment programs basically do two things well. First, they teach kids basic lessons about right and wrong ways to behave. Of course, there are other ways besides formally rewarding and punishing to teach these basic lessons, including *direct instruction*: "Don't touch the hot stove or you'll get burned." "If you don't share your toys, your friend won't want to play with you." "If you don't look both ways before crossing the street, you could get hurt." A lot of the teaching of basic lessons about right and wrong ways to behave is accomplished though direct instruction, and many kids (perhaps most) learn from and modify their behavior in response to this form of teaching.

Of course, some don't. Does it mean they need a formal reward and punishment program? No, not yet. If a kid doesn't benefit maximally from direct instruction, another very powerful and persuasive teaching tool inevitably kicks in next: *natural* consequences. There's a powerful natural consequence that occurs when one touches a hot stove, one that would teach a persuasive lesson. And there are powerful and persuasive natural consequences that occur if a kid doesn't share his toys or if he crosses the street without looking both ways. A lot of kids learn from and modify their behavior in response to natural consequences.

But then there are those who don't. Now are we ready for a formal reward and punishment program? Actually, we've now arrived at the fork in the road. If you've come to the conclusion that your kid, who hasn't benefited from the natural consequences, needs *even more* consequences, then you'll head in the direction of a formal reward and punishment program.

But what if you've concluded instead that the reason your kid hasn't responded to direct instruction or to those powerful and persuasive natural consequences is because he lacks crucial skills and has difficulty navigating certain unsolved problems? Will a formal reward and punishment program remediate the lagging skills that are setting the stage for his explosions or solve the problems that are reliably and predictably precipitating them? No, those are things reward and punishment programs don't do well at all. In my experience—perhaps yours, too—getting punished or not receiving an anticipated reward makes explosive kids more likely to explode, not less.

By the way, every explosive kid I've worked with already knew the basic lessons about right and wrong ways to behave. What they needed from the adults who were trying to help them was something rewards and punishments could not accomplish.

There's something else reward and punishment programs do well: they provide kids with *extrinsic* motivation. If you assume that a kid isn't doing well because he *doesn't want to*, then it makes perfect sense to provide motivation extrinsically—in other words, to *make him want to* by punishing the behaviors you want to discourage and rewarding the replacement behaviors you want to encourage.

Here's an interesting fact, and one you may find hard to believe: every explosive kid I've ever worked with was already motivated to do well. Kids do well if they can. They prefer doing well to not doing well. Consequences don't teach the skills explosive kids lack; they just increase the likelihood that a kid will exhibit skills he's *already capable* of consistently performing. Explosive kids don't need more consequences. They're already motivated to do well. They need something else from us.

Now you understand why, for the remainder of the book, we're going to take a different path. But first, let's go back and take a closer look at what happened when Amy's parents tried to implement formal reward and punishment procedures. They gave directions in a clearer way and put forth great effort to notice when Amy was behaving appropriately. They made a list of the behaviors Amy needed to improve on: brushing her teeth, doing her homework, coming in from playing outside, getting along with her younger brother, getting ready for school in the morning, and complying with adult directives. They kept track of how Amy was doing on these behaviors with a point system; she received points when she did well on a given behavior and lost points when she didn't do so well. The parents made a list of tangible rewards and special privileges Amy would earn when she had a sufficient number of points. If Amy failed to comply with adult directives, she was given a time-out. They were now quite certain that Amy was very motivated to do well.

The following scenario occurred countless times. After providing Amy with advance notice, the parents would give a direction; for example, "Amy, it's time to turn off the TV and go brush your teeth." In many instances, Amy—whose skills at shifting gears were not outstanding, no matter how much notice she received—wouldn't budge. The parents would repeat the directive. Amy would become certifiably frustrated. The parents would then calmly remind Amy of the consequences of failing to comply with their expectations and directives. Amy, who wasn't especially enthusiastic about losing points or ending up in time-out, would become more frustrated and increasingly disorganized and irrational, her control over her words and actions greatly diminished. She'd begin screaming and crying. Amy's parents would interpret her increased intensity and failure to respond to their directive as an attempt to force them to "back down" or "give in" and would inform her that a time-out was imminent. Amy would begin throwing things at her parents. Her parents would take Amy by the arm to escort her to time-out, an action that would intensify her frustration and irrationality even further. Amy would resist being placed in time-out and would try to scratch and claw her parents. They would try to restrain her physically in time-out (many clinicians no longer recommend this practice, but Amy's wasn't one of them); Amy would try to spit on or bite or head-butt them. They would confine Amy to her room until she calmed down. Once locked in her room—when her parents were actually able to get her there and keep her there—she would destroy anything she could get her hands on, including some of her favorite toys.

Eventually, anywhere from ten minutes to two hours later, Amy's explosion would peter out and rationality would be restored. Her exhausted, frustrated parents would hope that what they and their daughter just endured would eventually pay off in the form of improved compliance. When Amy would finally emerge from her room, she would be remorseful. The parents would, in a firm tone, reissue the direction that started the whole episode in the first place.

What's the matter with this picture? Quite a bit. If a child is delayed in reading, what's the appropriate intervention? Figure out why and teach the skills he lacks. If a child is delayed in the development of mathematics skills, what's the appropriate intervention? Figure out why and teach the skills he lacks. And if your child is challenged in the domains of flexibility, frustration tolerance, and problem solving, what should you do? Figure out why, teach the skills he lacks, and start solving the problems that are reliably and predictably precipitating his challenging episodes.

Q & A

Question: I've been being very firm with my child to make sure he knows I won't bend. But if he's inflexible, then is my inflexibility just making things worse?

Answer: Yes. There's a simple math equation to summarize this situation:

$$inflexibility + inflexibility = explosion$$

If your child is going to learn to be more flexible, to handle frustrations more adaptively, and to get better at solving problems, it's not going to happen if you're busy being a role model for inflexibility.

Question: Does that mean I have to say yes to everything just so my child doesn't explode?

Answer: It doesn't mean that at all.

Question: Don't I need to set a precedent so my child knows who's the boss?

Answer: Your child already knows you're the boss. Mission accomplished. He needs something else from you.

Question: So I'll still be in charge?

Answer: You're going to feel a lot more in charge than you do now.

6

Three Plans (One in Particular)

Now that we understand how your challenging kid came to be challenging, and that you know that sticker charts, time-outs, and re-warding and punishing don't teach the skills he's lacking or solve problems durably and therefore may not be what your kid needs, and now that you've identified four or five unsolved problems that are reliably and predictably precipitating your kid's challenging episodes, you're ready to learn about the Plans. Of all the chapters in this book, I'm told this is the one that people refer to over and over.

There are basically three ways to handle problems or unmet expectations. I call these options Plans, as in

Plan A, Plan B, and Plan C. It's important to emphasize that the Plans come into play only when there is an unsolved problem. If there is no problem, then you don't need a Plan. For example, if your child is completing his homework to your satisfaction and without significant difficulty or conflict, you don't need a Plan because there's not a problem to be solved. If your child is brushing his teeth to your satisfaction and without significant difficulty or conflict, you don't need a Plan because there is not a problem to be solved. But if your child is not completing his homework or brushing his teeth in accordance with your expectations, and if these problems heighten the likelihood of explosions, you need a Plan.

Plan A refers to handling a problem or unmet expectation through the *imposition of adult will*. Plan C involves *dropping an expectation completely*, at least for now. And Plan B involves doing *Collaborative Problem Solving*, a process by which you engage the child in resolving a problem in a mutually satisfactory manner. If you intend to follow the advice in this book, the Plans—one of them in particular—are your future. Let's take a closer look.

PLAN A

Many people think the terminology Plan A refers to the preferred plan. Not in this book. If you respond to an unsolved problem by imposing your will—by saying things like "No," "You must," or "You can't"—you're using Plan A. If your child often has trouble completing homework and you respond by insisting that the homework be completed, you're using Plan A. If your child often doesn't brush his teeth with the frequency or diligence you expect and you take away screen time until your expectation is met, you're using Plan A.

Now, these adult responses to unsolved problems might sound fairly ordinary, and they typically don't set the stage for challenging behavior if you have a fairly ordinary kid. You don't. In the case of explosive kids, Plan A—imposing your will—greatly heightens the likelihood of an explosion. Why? Because you're throwing Plan A at a kid who doesn't have a Plan A brain. Why doesn't he have a Plan A brain? None of us is especially enthusiastic about having someone else's will imposed on us. But most of us have the skills to handle having someone else's will imposed on us when it happens. Explosive kids don't. Recall from chapter 2 the conditions under which explosions occur: *whenever a kid doesn't have the skills to deal well with the demands that are being placed on him.* If you throw Plan A at a kid who doesn't have the skills to handle Plan A, you've placed a cognitive demand on him that outstrips his capacity to respond adaptively. That's why he's responding maladaptively. Indeed, when we "rewind the tape" on the vast majority of explosions in children, what we find is an adult using Plan A.

Now, an interesting paradox to ponder: Which kids get more Plan A thrown at them than any other type of kid? The explosive ones. The ones least capable of handling Plan A. That's because somewhere along the line many people became convinced that the best way to help explosive kids explode less and fully appreciate "who's the boss" was to apply massive doses of Plan A. Now you know that's actually the perfect recipe for massive numbers of explosions, a relationship with your kid that is distinctly unhelpful, and a kid who is wondering when his "boss" is going to start handling his difficulties in a new way that makes things better.

And that may be the most important point: Often, Plan A doesn't durably solve the homework problem or the toothbrushing problem. Nor does it help kids be more flexible, tolerate frustration more adaptively, or solve problems more effectively. It just sets the stage for more Plan A and more explosions.

If Plan A isn't working for you and your kid, I'd recommend you stop using it. Of course, if you stop using Plan A, you're going to need another way to deal with unmet expectations. That's Plan B. But we're not quite there yet. Let's go over Plan C first.

PLAN C

Plan C involves dropping some expectations completely, at least temporarily. Many people come to the instantaneous but erroneous conclusion that Plan C is the equivalent of "giving in." Actually, "giving in" is what happens when you start with Plan A and end up capitulating because your kid made your life miserable. When you deliberately use Plan C you're not capitulating; rather,

you've intentionally, thoughtfully, and proactively decided to drop a given expectation, either because you've
decided it was unrealistic in the first place or because
you have other, higher-priority expectations to pursue.
Temporarily dropping low-priority expectations can help
you and your kid to be more "available" to work on
higher-priority unsolved problems. The biggest downside to Plan C is that some expectations won't be met, at
least not yet. Of course, there's a major upside to Plan C:
any expectation you've dropped won't cause explosions
(if you've truly dropped it).

You're probably wondering which of your unmet expectations should end up on the back burner. That, of
course, depends on the specifics of your situation: your
priorities, your kid's level of instability, and how many
unsolved problems you think your kid (and you) can
work on at once. But toothbrushing, food choices, exer-
cising, doing homework, using good table manners, and
even getting to school on time and swearing sometimes
end up being handled with Plan C until more pressing
problems are resolved.

A few examples might help. One kid, Justin, was remarkably particular about what foods he was willing to
eat: certain cereals for breakfast and pizza for dinner.
Justin's parents were quite determined—as evidenced by
their relentless badgering and nagging (badgering and
nagging, by the way, are halfhearted forms of Plan A)—
that he have a balanced diet. This example of what could
be called *reciprocal inflexibility* led to at least two explosions a day (one each at breakfast and dinner). Except in

extreme cases, such as bona fide eating disorders, issues associated with diabetes, obesity, and so forth, a Plan C approach to food is usually indicated with picky-eating explosive kids. In other words, they won't starve. And, indeed, Justin wasn't starving. The expectation "eating a variety of foods" was initially handled with Plan C, explosions over this issue were eliminated, more pressing unsolved problems were addressed first, and the food problem was eventually addressed with Plan B. Over time, Justin began eating a somewhat wider variety of foods and then began accompanying his mother to the supermarket to make his own broader selections.

Another kid, Eduardo, routinely exploded whenever his mother brought him to the supermarket. Eduardo exploded in other situations as well, of course, but none as predictably as the supermarket. No matter what the mother tried—scolding, berating, punishing, rewarding—Eduardo still routinely exploded at the supermarket. These interventions weren't very effective at helping Eduardo master certain skills (staying next to the shopping cart, not demanding that his mother purchase every high-sugar cereal on the shelves, being patient in the checkout line) central to behaving well at the supermarket. His mother finally came to the conclusion that having Eduardo escort her to the supermarket was not essential. She decided he'd be much better off if she eliminated the expectation that her son accompany her to the supermarket (Plan C). Of course, his mother did have some concerns about placing this problem on the back burner.

Mother: But he can't avoid supermarkets forever, right?

Answer: Right. Luckily, going to the supermarket isn't critical to Eduardo's existence right now.

Mother: What about *my* existence? It's not always possible for his grandmother to watch him for me while I'm at the supermarket.

Answer: Yes, I understand. But it's even harder—and a lot more detrimental to your existence and your relationship with your son—to have him exploding every time you take him to the supermarket.

Mother: I don't know anyone else who can't bring her kid to the supermarket. This is ridiculous!

Answer: You're on a different playing field from people who don't have any trouble with their kids at the supermarket.

Mother: When should I try taking him into supermarkets again?

Answer: When you think he can do it . . . and when you've learned how to use Plan B.

PLAN B

Plan B involves doing Collaborative Problem Solving (CPS), a process by which you and your child work together—collaborate—to solve the problems that have been setting the stage for explosions and that have been so destructive to your relationship with each other.

Fair warning: according to many popular parenting books—and the conventional wisdom—you should never collaborate with a child. After all, you're in charge. But in this book, being "in charge" means that you understand why, with this particular child, even the most mundane of problems can set the stage for explosions, and that you're willing to take action to change course. Don't worry, you're still in charge when you're using Plan B, probably more in charge than you've ever been. The only down side to Plan B is that, at least initially, it's hard to do, but mostly because many people haven't had much practice with it.

Plan B consists of three ingredients. The first, called the *Empathy step*, involves gathering information from your child to understand his concern or perspective on a given unsolved problem. The second, called the *Define the Problem step*, involves communicating your concern or perspective on the same unsolved problem. And the third—the *Invitation*—is when you and your child discuss and agree on a solution that will address each other's concerns. These three ingredients are crucial to the collaborative resolution of a problem.

CPS is not a "technique" or a "quick-fix" that will magically or totally transform a child in a snap. CPS is a process, one that cannot be achieved overnight. The goals of solving problems durably, teaching skills, and changing fundamental aspects of the way you interact with your child are not going to be achieved in a week.

On first hearing about Plan B, many people come to the erroneous conclusion that the best time to use Plan B is just as they are in the midst of dealing with an unsolved problem. That's Emergency Plan B, and it's actually not the best timing because the child is already heated up. Few of us do our clearest thinking when we're heated up. As discussed earlier, the problems precipitating most explosions are highly predictable. Thus, there's no reason to wait until the child gets heated up yet again to try to solve problems that have been causing explosions for a very long time. The goal is to get the problem solved—ahead of time—before it comes up again. That's Proactive Plan B. For example, if your child always balks at brushing his teeth, the best time to have a Plan B discussion with him is before he's faced with the task of toothbrushing again rather than in the heat of the moment. If your child routinely has difficulty with his homework, the time to have a Plan B discussion aimed at solving that problem is before he's struggling with his homework the next time. Let's sink our teeth into the three ingredients and then think more about how best to apply them, preferably proactively.

THE EMPATHY STEP

The goal of the Empathy step is to *gather information from your kid to achieve the clearest possible understanding of his concern or perspective on a given unsolved problem.* Just like adults, kids have legitimate concerns: hunger, fatigue, fear, the desire to buy or do certain things, the tendency to avoid things that are scary or that make them uncomfortable or at which they don't feel competent.

Many adults have some interesting reactions when they read or hear about the Empathy step. Some never considered understanding their kid's concerns or perspective on things to be particularly important. That's why many kids—perhaps most—are accustomed to having their concerns dismissed (by adults who have concerns of their own). Dismissing kids' concerns isn't ideal to begin with, but if you dismiss an *explosive* kid's concerns, he's going to explode. And that's not the only downside. If you're busy dismissing your kid's concerns, don't be surprised when he reciprocates. If you don't understand the concerns that are fueling explosions, then those concerns won't get addressed and the explosions will persist. By the way, you don't lose any authority by gathering information, understanding, and empathizing. Rather, you gain a problem-solving partner.

When you're using Proactive Plan B, the information-gathering and understanding process begins with a neutral observation (usually starting with the words "I've noticed that . . .") about one of the items from your list of unsolved problems and continues with an initial inquiry (something like, "What's up?"). Here are some common examples:

"I've noticed that you haven't been too enthusiastic about going to school lately. What's up?"

"I've noticed that we've been arguing a lot lately about toothbrushing. What's up?"

"I've noticed that homework's been a real struggle for us lately. What's up?"

"I've noticed that we've been arguing a lot about how much time you're spending playing video games. What's up?"

"I've noticed that we've been fighting a lot about your bedtime. What's up?"

"I've noticed that it's been hard for you to wake up in the morning to get to school lately. What's up?"

"I've noticed that you've been missing the school bus a lot. What's up?"

It's important to take note of the neutral aspect of the neutral observation. Here are some examples of observations that aren't neutral at all:

"I've noticed you're trying to ruin my life. What's up?"

"I've noticed you don't care about school anymore. Well, if you don't care, I don't care."

"I've noticed you're not interested in doing your homework anymore. I guess you'll have to learn the hard way."

"I've noticed you don't want to wake up in the morning for school. So I'm taking your Wii away until that improves."

Aside from setting the stage for explosions, these non-neutral observations are counterproductive because they cause kids to stop talking. If your main mission is to gather information to understand a kid's concern or perspective about a given unsolved problem, then you don't want him to stop talking. If he stops talking, his concern or perspective won't get addressed and the explosions over that problem will continue.

Of course, the neutral observation and inquiry are just the beginning of the Empathy step. After you ask "What's up?" your child is going to respond. He may, for example, respond with "I don't know." Now, "I don't know" can mean many different things, and it will be important for you to figure out what "I don't know" means in your kid's case (I discuss this in great detail in the next chapter). For now, let's assume that "I don't know" means your kid has never given the matter much thought and needs some time to think, in which case you'd simply want to respond with patience and encouragement, perhaps by saying "I guess I've never asked you about this before. Take your time. We're not in a rush."

Another potential response to "What's up?" is silence, which tends to be a bit disquieting to many adults, who have a tendency to fill the void with the sound of their own voices. Often, rather than giving the child time to collect his thoughts, the adult talks ("I think the reason you're spending so much time in front of your video game is because you don't want to do your chores"). In such instances, you've strayed quite a bit from seeking information and made it even more difficult for your kid to think. You may need to grow more comfortable with the silence that can occur as a kid is giving thought to his concerns.

Even when your child's first response to "What's up?" provides some useful information, it's not enough to provide you with a clear understanding of his concern or perspective, so you're going to need to drill for more information. Notice, the word is "drill," not "grill." The primary goal of drilling is to *clarify*, whereas grilling tends to be an act of intimidation. Your goal here is to demonstrate to your child that your attempt to understand his concern or perspective isn't perfunctory—*you really want to understand*. This is the hardest part of the Empathy step, mostly because (1) adults are overconfident that they already know what a kid's concern or perspective is, and (2) even when they aren't so confident, they also aren't exactly sure what to say to clarify a kid's concerns. In regard to (1), my experience is that adults are frequently wrong about a kid's concerns. In regard to (2), clarifying your kid's concerns usually involves focusing on the who, what, where, when, and why of an unsolved problem, along with questions and statements like "How so?" "Say more," "I'm confused," "Can you tell me more about that?" "I don't quite understand," and "I don't get it."

Here's an example:

Parent: I've noticed that we've been struggling a lot over homework lately. What's up?"

Kid: It's too hard.

Parent: It's too hard . . . which part is too hard?

Kid: It's too much.

Parent: It's too much. I don't understand . . . what's too much?

Kid: The writing part is too much.

Parent: Ah, the writing part is too much. Is the writing part hard on everything?

Kid: No.

Parent: On what parts of your homework is the writing part too much?

Kid: I don't know.

Parent: Well, take your time. We're not in a rush.

Kid: It's not the spelling . . . all I have to do is write one word.

Parent: So that's not it.

Kid: And it's not the social studies. All I have to do is draw a line from one word to another.

Parent: Hmm.

Kid: It's the science part. Mrs. Moore is making us write entire paragraphs! It's too hard!

Parent: Ah, it's the science homework. Yes, Mrs. Moore is making you write entire paragraphs.

Kid: It's too much! It's too hard!

Parent: Well, I'm glad we're figuring this out. But I'm

still a little confused. What is it about writing the
entire paragraphs that is so hard for you?

Kid: You know I'm a slow writer! It takes me so long
to write the words that I forget what I wanted to
say. So then I just get all mad and then I stop
doing my homework.

Interesting. By drilling, we went all the way from "It's too hard" to "It takes me so long to write the words that I forget what I wanted to say" and came away with a much clearer sense of the problem that needs to be solved. If we don't have the clearest possible sense of the kid's concerns, the problem won't get solved.

Adults are often astounded at what they learn when they start inquiring about a kid's concerns. Let's see what information turns up with the other examples from above (all of which would then require further drilling):

Adult: I've noticed that you haven't been too
enthusiastic about going to school lately. What's up?

Kid: Sophie's been hitting me on the playground.

Adult: I've noticed that we've been arguing a lot
lately about toothbrushing. What's up?

Kid: I don't like the taste of the toothpaste.

Adult: I've noticed that we've been arguing a lot
about how much time you're spending playing
video games. What's up?

Kid: I don't have anyone to play with. No one in the neighborhood wants to play with me.

Adult: I've noticed that we've been fighting a lot about your bedtime. What's up?
Kid: I don't like being alone in the dark.

Adult: I've noticed that it's been hard for you to wake up in the morning to get to school lately. What's up?
Kid: Ever since we started that new medicine, I'm really tired in the morning.

Adult: I've noticed that you've been missing the school bus a lot. What's up?
Kid: I don't want to take the school bus anymore. The bus driver always blames me when there's trouble.

Some adults, having now made some headway toward understanding their kids' concerns, have difficulty resisting the temptation to revert to form by being dismissive or using Plan A, thereby ending the conversation. Here are some examples of what *not* to do:

Adult: I've noticed that you haven't been too enthusiastic about going to school lately. What's up?
Kid: Sophie's been hitting me on the playground.
Adult: Well, you should just hit her back.

Adult: I've noticed that we've been arguing a lot lately about toothbrushing. What's up?

Kid: I don't like the taste of the toothpaste.

Adult: I don't like the taste of the toothpaste either, but that doesn't stop me from brushing my teeth.

Adult: I've noticed that we've been arguing a lot about how much time you're spending playing video games. What's up?

Kid: I don't have anyone to play with. No one in the neighborhood wants to play with me.

Adult: Oh, you have lots of friends. I think you're just making excuses.

Adult: I've noticed that we've been fighting a lot about your bedtime. What's up?

Kid: I don't like being alone in the dark.

Adult: Oh, you'll be fine.

Adult: I've noticed that it's been hard for you to wake up in the morning to get to school lately. What's up?

Kid: Ever since we started that new medicine, I'm really tired in the morning.

Adult: I think you just need to try harder.

Adult: I've noticed that you've been missing the school bus a lot. What's up?

Kid: I don't want to take the school bus anymore. The bus driver always blames me when there's trouble.

Adult: So just stay away from the kids who cause trouble and the bus driver won't blame you.

Two more points about the Empathy step before we move on. You may have noticed that while this first step is called the Empathy step, your primary goal is not necessarily to empathize by saying something like "Oh, that must be very hard for you." It's not a crime to say something empathic; it's just that empathic statements don't typically elicit the information you're seeking.

You may be wondering if your kid has sufficient language-processing skills to participate in Plan B. There's no question that the examples above show what Plan B looks like with kids who have these skills. In later chapters I describe modifications for kids who are having difficulty participating in Plan B because of poor communication skills or for a variety of other reasons.

THE DEFINE THE PROBLEM STEP

You're ready to move on to the Define the Problem step when you have a clear understanding of your kid's concern or perspective on a given unsolved problem. The primary goal of the Define the Problem step is to enter your concern or perspective into consideration. The name of this step derives from the fact that in Collaborative Problem Solving a problem is defined by two concerns that have yet to be reconciled: the kid's and yours. The Define the Problem step usually begins with the words "My concern is . . ." or "The thing is . . ."

This step is made difficult primarily by the fact that, like kids, adults often don't give much thought to their *concerns* about specific problems. It's quite common for adults, in their eagerness to get the problem solved, to jet past their concerns and land the plane on their *solutions*. And because kids have a tendency to do the exact same thing (perhaps they've been well trained), the typical scenario is something called *dueling solutions*, also known as a power struggle:

Adult: Is your homework done?

Kid: My homework's too hard.

Adult: Your homework's too hard? It's getting late. Go do it. Now!

Kid: It's too hard! I'm not doing it! (*Kid's solution*)

Adult: Oh, you're doing it all right! Now! (*Adult's solution*)

Kaboom. Concerns not clarified. Problem not solved. Fortunately, solving problems collaboratively isn't about power. Nor is it about struggling, though it is hard. It's about clarifying the concerns of both parties and then working toward solutions that address those concerns. You're not ready to think about solutions until the concerns of both parties have been clarified (otherwise, you don't know what problem you're really trying to solve). So you'll need to give some careful thought to your concerns. If you're having difficulty figuring out what your concern is about a given problem, here's some good news: It's probably not that complicated. The vast majority of adult concerns are related to safety, or health, or how your kid's behavior is affecting him or others.

Let's see what some typical adult concerns might be on some of the problems we considered above:

Not going to school: *The thing is, if you don't go to school, I'm concerned that you're going to miss out on a lot of important learning. Plus, we wouldn't really be solving the problem of Sophie's hitting you.*

Toothbrushing: *The thing is, if you don't brush your teeth, you're going to get cavities and I'm going to have to spend a lot of money on the dentist.*

Homework: *My concern is that you're missing out on a lot of important practice—and getting lower grades—by not doing your homework.*

Video games: *My concern is that all that time alone in front of the video games isn't making it any more likely that the other kids will want to play with you. And it's making it harder for you to get around to your chores.*

Bedtime: *The thing is, when we argue about your bedtime, you end up going to bed really late, and then you're really tired in the morning.*

Waking up: *My concern is that you're falling behind in your first two classes because you've been late to school so often.*

Missing the school bus: *My concern is that when you miss the school bus, I have to take you to school myself, and my boss is getting a little upset about me coming in late.*

Let's now continue the example of Proactive Plan B we began above, with the Define the Problem Step added:

Parent: I've noticed that we've been struggling a lot over homework lately. What's up?

Kid: It's too hard.

Parent: It's too hard. Which part is too hard?

Kid: It's too much.

Parent: It's too much. I don't understand. What's too much?

Kid: The writing part is too much.

Parent: Ah, the writing part is too much. Is the writing part hard on everything?

Kid: No.

Parent: On what parts of your homework is the writing part too much?

Kid: I don't know.

Parent: Well, take your time. We're not in a rush.

Kid: It's not the spelling . . . all I have to do is write one word.

Parent: So that's not it.

Kid: And it's not the social studies. All I have to do is draw a line from one word to another.

Parent: Hmm.

Kid: It's the science part. Mrs. Moore is making us write entire paragraphs! It's too hard!

Parent: Ah, it's the science homework. Yes, Mrs. Moore is making you write entire paragraphs.

Kid: It's too much! It's too hard!

Parent: Well, I'm glad we're figuring this out. But I'm still a little confused. What is it about writing the entire paragraphs that is so hard for you?

Kid: You know I'm a slow writer! It takes me so long to write the words that I forget what I wanted to say. So then I just get all mad and then I stop doing my homework.

Parent: So it takes you so long to write the words that you forget what you wanted to say. I understand. The thing is, if you stop doing your homework completely, then you won't get any practice at the writing and it will always be hard for you.

Two concerns are on the table. No turning back now.

THE INVITATION STEP

This final step involves brainstorming potential solutions to a now well-defined problem. So I should have called this the Brainstorming step. But I called it the Invitation step because the adult actually invites the child to solve the problem collaboratively. The Invitation lets the child know that solving the problem is something you're doing *with* him—together—rather than *to* him. To do this, you could simply say something like "Let's think about how we can solve this problem" or "Let's think about how we can work that out." But to make things as explicit as possible, I recommend that you recap the two concerns that were identified in the first two steps, usually starting with the words "I wonder if there's a way." So, in the above example, that would sound something like this: "I wonder if there's a way for us to help you with the writing part so it doesn't take so long and make you so mad . . ." (that was the kid's concern) ". . . but still give you some practice at it so it won't always be so hard for you" (that was the adult's concern).

Then you give the kid the first crack at generating a solution ("Do you have any ideas?"). This is not an indication that the burden for solving the problem is placed solely on the kid. The burden for solving the problem is placed on the Problem-Solving Team: your child and you. But giving your kid the first crack at thinking of a solution can be a good strategy, for it lets him know you're actually interested in his ideas.

Many parents, in their eagerness to solve the problem, forget the Invitation. This means that just as they are at the precipice of actually collaborating with their child, they impose their will. Too often we assume that the only person capable of coming up with a good solution to a problem is the adult. While there is some chance that your kid won't be able to think of any solutions (an issue discussed in greater detail in chapter 7), there's actually an outstanding chance your child *can* think of good solutions, ones that will take your combined concerns into account. And there's a good chance he has been waiting (not so patiently) for you to give him the chance. So, as it relates to solving problems with your child, here's an important theme: *Don't be a "genius."*

It's not terrible to have some ideas about how a problem can be solved, so long as you remember that Plan B is not simply a "clever" form of Plan A. When you use Plan B, you do so with the understanding that the solution is not predetermined. One father who had failed to remember this said, "I don't use Plan B unless I already know how the problem is going to be solved." If you already know how the problem is going to be solved before the discussion takes place, then you're not using Plan B—you're using a "clever" form of Plan A.

Though it seems like the notion that they're no longer responsible for coming up with an instantaneous, ingenious solution to a problem would be welcome, it takes some getting used to for many adults. Most problems aren't solved in a nanosecond. Most problems that are solved in a nanosecond aren't durably solved anyway. Solving a difficult problem durably requires reflection, consideration, time, a willingness to let the process of exploring solutions unfold, and, most of all, collaboration. If you're thinking that Plan B can sometimes take a long time, you're right. But explosions take much longer.

This next part is crucial. Each solution under consideration is evaluated on the basis of whether it is *realistic* and *mutually satisfactory*. If a solution isn't realistic and mutually satisfactory, the problem isn't solved yet and the Problem-Solving Team is still working on it.

The realistic part is important because Plan B isn't an exercise in wishful thinking. If you can't execute your part of the solution that's under consideration, don't agree to it just to end the conversation. Likewise, if you don't think your kid can execute his part of the solution that's under consideration, then try to get him to take a moment to think about whether he can actually do what he's agreeing to do. ("You sure you can do that? Let's make sure we come up with a solution we can both do.") By the way, "trying harder" is seldom a viable solution.

The mutually satisfactory part is important, too, and is of great comfort to adults who fear that in using Plan B their concerns will go unaddressed and no limits will be set. You're "setting limits" if your concerns are being addressed. If a solution is mutually satisfactory, then by definition your concerns have been addressed. So if you thought that Plan A is the only mechanism by which adults can set limits, you were mistaken. If your concerns are being addressed with Plan B, then why do you still need Plan A? Maybe you don't.

The mutually satisfactory part also helps kids stop exploding. If a kid's concerns are being heard, clarified, understood, validated, and addressed, rather than dismissed or ignored, and if problems are being solved collaboratively, rather than through imposition of adult will, then there may really be nothing left to explode about.

Early on, many kids have a tendency to think of solutions that will address *their* concerns but not *yours* (many adults have the same tendency). But if you want him to be thinking rather than exploding, the last thing you'd want to do is tell him he's come up with a bad idea. Instead, simply remind him that the goal is to come up with a solution that works for both of you, perhaps by saying, "Well, that's an idea . . . and I know that idea would address your concern . . . but I don't think it would address my concern. Let's see if we can come up with an idea that will work for both of us." In other words, there's no such thing as a bad solution—only solutions that aren't realistic or mutually satisfactory. *Your goal—and this is very important—is to prove to your kid that you are as invested in making sure that his concern is addressed as you are in making sure that yours is addressed.*

Let's see how the three ingredients would go together, assuming that things are going smoothly (we'll get to problems people encounter in using Plan B soon enough):

Parent: I've noticed that we've been struggling a lot over homework lately. What's up?"

Kid: It's too hard.

Parent: It's too hard. Which part is too hard?

Kid: It's too much.

Parent: It's too much. I don't understand. What's too much?

Kid: The writing part is too much.

Parent: Ah, the writing part is too much. Is the writing part hard on everything?

Kid: No.

Parent: On what parts of your homework is the writing part too much?

Kid: I don't know.

Parent: Well, take you're time. We're not in a rush.

Kid: It's not the spelling . . . all I have to do is write one word.

Parent: So that's not it.

Kid: And it's not the social studies. All I have to do is draw a line from one word to another.

Parent: Hmm.

Kid: It's the science part. Mrs. Moore is making us write entire paragraphs! It's too hard!

Parent: Ah, it's the science homework. Yes, Mrs. Moore is making you write entire paragraphs.

Kid: It's too much! It's too hard!

Parent: Well, I'm glad we're figuring this out. But I'm still a little confused. What is it about writing the entire paragraphs that is so hard for you?

Kid: You know I'm a slow writer! It takes me so long to write the words that I forget what I wanted to say. So then I just get all mad and then I stop doing my homework.

Parent: So it takes you so long to write the words that you forget what you wanted to say. I understand. The thing is, if you stop doing your homework completely, then you won't get any practice at the writing and it will always be hard for you.

Parent: I wonder if there's a way for us to help you with the writing part so it doesn't take so long and make you so mad but still give you some practice at it so it won't always be so hard for you. Do you have any ideas?

Kid: Um . . . no.

Parent: Well, take your time. We've never really talked about it like this before. If you don't have any ideas, maybe I can come up with some.

Kid: If we could just come up with a way for me to remember what I wanted to write, then maybe I wouldn't get so frustrated.

Parent: Let's think about that. How could we help you remember what you wanted to write?

Kid: At school, sometimes they have someone scribe for me.

Parent: I know, but the last time I asked if I could scribe for you, they said they wanted you to practice your writing on your homework. Of course, they don't know what we go through around here during homework. I could ask them again, but I wonder if there's any other way we could help you remember what you wanted to write.

Kid: I could say what I wanted to write into your voice recorder. You know how you do for work? Then I could just play the recording back and write it down.

Parent: That could work. That would make it easier for you to remember what you want to write?

Kid: I think so.

Parent: Well, it sounds like that solution works for you, and it certainly works for me. I don't use my voice recorder when you're doing your homework, so it sounds realistic. Shall we give it a try?

Kid: Okay.

Parent: And if that solution doesn't work, we'll talk some more and come up with one that does.

Kid: Okay.

The parent's last line was significant, as it underscores a very important point: It's good for the kid and adult to acknowledge that the problem may require additional discussion, because there's actually a decent chance that *the first solution won't solve the problem durably.* Why wouldn't the first solution solve the problem durably? Often because the solution wasn't as realistic or mutually satisfactory as it first seemed. Or because the first attempt at clarifying concerns yielded useful but incomplete information. And because, in real life, solving problems that have been causing major disagreements for a long time isn't a one-shot deal. Good solutions—durable ones—are usually variants of the solutions that came before them.

It's also important to mention that Plan B isn't usually this easy, especially early on. For example, sometimes kids (and even adults) get pretty heated up while using Plan B. Sometimes this is because history has taught them that disagreements are always handled using Plan A. It may take a while (and a lot of Plan B) for the child's instantaneous heated reaction to unsolved problems to subside. Adults sometimes become impatient in the midst of Plan B and head for Plan A or Plan C. Hang in there.

There's much more to cover about Plan B, but you've been given a lot to digest already. And upon first reading

about the Plans, many adults have some misconceptions.
Let's get a few things cleared up before they cause trouble.

Q & A

Question: Let me get this straight: I'm supposed to drop
all my expectations so my kid doesn't explode anymore?

Answer: Far from it. Dropping an expectation, at least
temporarily, is Plan C. And while Plan C can be an important part of stabilizing things—because it removes
some of the unsolved problems that have been causing
explosions—Plan B is the new way you're going to try
to solve problems so your expectations are met. Remember, if a solution to a problem is mutually satisfactory, then your concerns have been addressed.

Question: Isn't this just about picking battles?

Answer: It is if your only options are Plan A and Plan
C. And, sadly, "battle picking" is the uncomfortable
position many parents—especially those who don't
know about Plan B—find themselves in: impose adult
will and cause an explosion (Plan A), or drop the
expectation and avoid an explosion (Plan C). Actually, under those conditions, Plan C is more an act of
desperation. When you add Plan B to the mix, you're
not picking battles anymore (because you're not battling anymore), and Plan C isn't an act of desperation
anymore. It's a planned, thoughtful, active effort to

remove some expectations and reduce explosions so you and your kid are more "available" to work collaboratively on the unsolved problems that remain.

Question: So I'm not allowed to tell my kid what to do anymore?

Answer: Telling your kid what to do—in other words, reminding him of an expectation—is probably fine. Unless you're finding that you're telling him what to do over and over again (and thereby heightening the likelihood of explosions). In that case, what you keep telling him to do (to brush his teeth, get ready for school, start his homework, do his chores, and so forth) qualifies as an unsolved problem, and all that "telling" clearly isn't helping you and your child move any closer toward a durable, mutually satisfactory solution. And, of course, if your particular style of "telling" includes screaming, berating, belittling, or threats . . . well, those embellishments move things even further in the wrong direction. You might want to give Plan B a good try.

Question: So the problems I really care about, that's Plan A. And the problems I sort of care about, that's Plan B. And the problems I don't care about at all, that's Plan C. Yes?

Answer: No. The Plans are not a ranking system. Each Plan represents a distinct way of responding to unsolved problems. With Plan A, you're imposing your will and greatly heightening the likelihood of an explosion. With Plan C, you're dropping the expectation completely, at least temporarily, and reducing the likelihood of an explosion. And with Plan B, you're clarifying concerns and working out solutions that are realistic and mutually satisfactory and solving problems durably, so they don't cause explosions anymore.

Question: You said there was a decent chance my kid wouldn't have any ideas for solutions once we arrived at the Invitation. I know you're talking about that later, but any quick tips?

Answer: Well, you're going to want to give him time to think. After all, there's an excellent chance the problem has never been well clarified and that he's never given thought to solutions that would address his and your concerns. And, of course, solutions you might offer will be an important part of the process, too. But more detail on this is just a few pages away.

Question: This is very hard work, isn't it?

Answer: Yes, it is. Of course, you're working hard already. Let's make sure you have something to show for all that hard work.

Question: I understand that Proactive Plan B is preferable to Emergency Plan B. But I'm still curious about what Emergency Plan B sounds like.

Answer: Emergency Plan B differs from Proactive Plan B on two counts: the timing and the wording of the

Empathy step. Because Emergency Plan B typically occurs in hurried conditions and after a kid is already heated up, it isn't ideal for gathering information and solving problems durably. So, while Emergency Plan B is available to you as an option, you don't want to make a habit of it. The Define the Problem step and the Invitation step are much the same with Emergency Plan B as with Proactive Plan B (though they're often louder and more intense under emergent conditions). And though the goal of the Empathy step is the same—information gathering and understanding—in Emergency Plan B, the Empathy step involves *reflective listening* rather than a neutral observation. Here are a few examples of what reflective listening would sound like:

Kid: I'm not taking my meds.
Adult: You're not taking your meds. What's up?

Kid: I'm not going to school today.
Adult: You're not going to school today. What's up?

Kid: This homework sucks!
Adult: You're getting frustrated about your
   homework. What's up?

Now, a caveat: while as a general rule Proactive Plan B is far preferable to Emergency Plan B, there are some kids—they are few and far between but they exist—who have difficulty participating in Proactive Plan B because they have trouble remembering the specifics of problems you're trying to discuss. For these kids, the problem is only memorable and salient when they're in the midst of it. Early on, Emergency Plan B may actually be preferable for these kids. I've found that many of these kids are able to participate in proactive discussions once Plan B becomes more familiar to them.

In chapter 3, you were given your first homework assignment: make a list of the problems that are routinely causing your child to become frustrated. Here's your next assignment: pick one of those problems and try using Proactive Plan B to solve it. If it goes well, terrific. If it doesn't go well—and since this is a new skill, there's a decent chance it won't—keep reading.

Here's a brief summary of what you've just read:

- There are three options for responding to unsolved problems: imposing your will (Plan A); dropping the expectation completely, at least for now (Plan C); and working out a solution that is realistic and mutually satisfactory (Plan B). With Plan A, you're greatly heightening the likelihood of an explosion. With Plan C, you're eliminating the potential for an explosion. With Plan B, you're reducing the likelihood of an explosion and solving the problem.

- Plan B consists of three steps or ingredients:

  > gathering information about and understanding your child's concern on a given problem (the Empathy step);

  > being specific about your concern or perspective on the same problem (the Define the Problem step); and

  > brainstorming with your child to find solutions that are realistic and mutually satisfactory (the Invitation).

- There are two forms of Plan B, depending on timing: Emergency Plan B and Proactive Plan B. Because Proactive Plan B is far preferable, it's been the primary focus of this chapter. Emergency Plan B—because of added heat and time pressure—is much harder and much less likely to lead to durable solutions.

- In Proactive Plan B, the Empathy step begins by making a neutral observation ("I've noticed that . . .") about one of the problems from your list of unsolved problems, followed by an inquiry ("What's up?"). Keep drilling until you feel you have a clear understanding of your kid's concern or perspective on the problem. The Define the Problem step usually begins with the words "My concern is . . ."

or "The thing is . . ." (you may want to give some thought to your concern or perspective on the problem ahead of time). In the Invitation ("I wonder if there's a way . . .") you should try to summarize the concerns that have been clarified in the first two steps and then give the kid the first crack at generating solutions. You aren't ready to begin thinking about solutions until you've clarified the concerns of both parties. I've created a Plan B "Cheat Sheet" to provide a concise reminder of these key points. You can find it at www.explosivechild.com.

- Like any new skill, Plan B is hard, and it takes time to get good at it. The more you practice, the easier Plan B becomes. Plan B isn't something you do two or three times before returning to your old way of doing things. It's not a technique; it's a way of life.

7

Trouble in Paradise

In chapter 6, you learned about your three options for responding to problems or unmet expectations, and a lot about one of those options (Plan B). You were also given your second homework assignment: try to solve a problem using Proactive Plan B.

How did your first attempt at Plan B go? If your answer is "not so bad," that's great. Now let's hope the solution you agreed to in Plan B stands the test of time. If the solution doesn't durably solve the problem, you'll find out soon enough. Then it's back to Plan B to figure out why and to come up with a solution that is more realistic or mutually satisfactory than the first one, or one that includes information that may not have been available in your first try. When you think the time is right, move on to another problem on the list.

But if your answer is "not well at all," don't despair. As you already know, it can take a while for you and your child to become good at this. And Plan B can go astray for a variety of reasons. Let's take a closer look at the patterns that may be getting in the way.

You're still not convinced that your explosive kid lacks the skills to be flexible, handle frustration, and solve problems.

You may want to go back and reread chapters 3 and 5. Don't forget, the alternative explanation—that your child is attention-seeking, manipulative, coercive, limit-testing, unmotivated, and so forth—hasn't made things any better, so you really don't have a lot to lose by trying a different explanation on for size.

You haven't done Plan B yet. You're still using Plan A and Plan C instead.

Maybe you don't feel very confident about your Plan B skills, so you're a little reluctant to give it a whirl. That's understandable. Or perhaps you're worried that your child will have a heated response to Plan B just as he's always had a heated response to Plan A. We can't rule out that possibility completely; some kids are so accustomed to Plan A that they don't immediately recognize that you're trying hard to understand their concerns and solve problems collaboratively. So you may have some "residual heat" to contend with. On the other hand, the Empathy step is very powerful, especially if you're using Plan B proactively rather than emergently. It comes down to this: if you never give Plan B a try, then you and your kid will never become good at it. No one is great at Plan B in the beginning. You and your child are becoming good at this together.

Of course, if you *intend* to drop an unsolved problem, at least temporarily, then Plan C is exactly what you should be using. And, as you've read, if you find yourself in an emergent safety situation then Plan A may make perfect sense at that moment. But, again, if it's a predictable safety issue, you don't want to rely solely on Plan A . . . you'll also want to use Proactive Plan B to solve the problem that's giving rise to the unsafe behavior in the first place.

You're using Emergency Plan B instead of Proactive Plan B.

Remember, when you're trying to solve a problem collaboratively, the time constraints and heat that go along with Emergency Plan B are working against you. Waiting for a predictable problem to arise again is not the ideal strategy for problem solving. You have better odds if you're trying to solve problems proactively, before they come up again.

You're not the methodical, organized type? That could be a problem because it may mean you're perpetually in crisis mode. Changing your relationship with your kid, solving problems collaboratively, and helping him learn the skills he needs to be more flexible and handle frustration more adaptively isn't going to be easy, and is likely to require that you make some adjustments to your standard operating procedure. So, at the very least, you're probably going to need to put some extra effort into being more proactive in generating a list of unsolved problems, prioritizing, and using Plan B.

You're busy? You're accustomed to living life in the fast lane and solving problems in the spur of the moment? That's fantastic, but you're leaving your kid floundering in your wake, and he's not doing well back there. We could demand that *he* adapt to *you*, but since flexibility and adaptability are not his strengths, the more realistic option is for *you* to adapt to *him*. Once he learns some skills and you are able to solve some chronic problems together, maybe he'll be able to reciprocate.

You're using Plan B as a last resort.

Plan B isn't an act of desperation, and it's not something you turn to only when your child is on the verge of exploding. Plan B requires forethought. And Plan A is not the ideal way to segue into Plan B.

You've been entering Plan B with a preordained solution.

It's fine to have some ideas for how a problem can be solved, but if you already know what the solution is before the discussion begins, you're using Plan A, not Plan B.

You've been suggesting solutions before clarifying concerns.

Remember, you don't know what problem you're really trying to solve until two concerns—yours and your kid's—have been identified.

You've been agreeing to solutions that aren't realistic and mutually satisfactory.

Better to take the time to broaden the range of solutions under consideration than to agree on a solution that's only going to precipitate an explosion later.

You've been trying to bake the cake without one of the three key ingredients.

Each of the three ingredients, each step, is indispensable in the collaborative resolution of a problem. If you skip the Empathy step, your child will think you're about to impose your will (Plan A) because you're leading off with your concern. Plan A slams the door on gathering information about your child's concern or perspective, meaning his concern or perspective won't get addressed and the problem won't get solved. Case in point:

A mother who had been trying Plan B for about three weeks arrived at the counselor's office one day with a common complaint.

"Plan B isn't working," she said.

"Tell me what happened," said the counselor.

"Well," said the mother, "on Tuesday I told Jeremy that I wanted to make sure he got his homework done before his karate class and asked him how we could work that out."

"So your concern was that he wouldn't get his homework done before his karate class," said the counselor.

"Right. I know that if he doesn't do his homework before his karate class, it's not going to get done because by the time we get home from his karate class he's too tired."

"That makes sense," said the counselor. "And what problem was it that you were trying to solve?"

"What problem were we trying to solve?" asked the mother, a little perplexed. "How we were going to get his homework done before his karate class."

"What was Jeremy's concern?" asked the counselor.

"His concern?" asked the mother, still confused.

"Yes, at the moment I'm hearing only your concern, which is that you were worried that he wouldn't get his homework done, and your solution, which is that he do his homework before karate class. What was his concern?"

"I didn't know he had a concern," said the mother.

"I'm wondering if that's because you skipped the first

step of Plan B, you know, the Empathy step," the counselor said.

"I knew I was doing something wrong!" said the mother.

"No one does very well at this in the beginning," said the counselor. "What happened when you told him your concern and invited him to solve the problem with you?"

"He started screaming at me," said the mother.

"Sounds like he must have had a concern, and that your solution didn't take it into account. The problem is, when you don't gather information about his concern and jump right to your concern, he thinks you're using Plan A."

"So what should I have said?" asked the mother.

"Well, as we've discussed, the Empathy step starts with a neutral observation and inquiry about a problem and continues with you drilling a little to clarify his concern. Maybe something like, 'I've noticed that we've been struggling over homework lately on days when you have karate. What's up?' Do you have any ideas about what concern he might have had about doing his homework before his karate class? Has this come up before?"

"Oh, it comes up all the time," said the mother. "That's why I was trying to solve it. He says he needs a break before he does his homework."

"Why does he need a break?" asked the counselor.

"Well, he's been in school all day—this is what he says. To tell you the truth, I don't know how hard he's actually working in school. Anyway, he always seems to have enough energy for karate . . ."

"But I suppose it makes some sense that if he's been in school for six hours, he might need a break before he jumps right into homework," said the counselor. "Sounds like a valid concern to me, if that's what his concern actually is."

The mother pondered the point. "I suppose so."

"So, are you ready to give it another try this week?" asked the counselor.

"This is hard!" said the mother.

The counselor nodded. "It does take some getting used to. But we don't want you to miss out on the good stuff the Empathy step brings to the mix. The truth is, it's impossible to solve the problem durably and in a way that works for both of you without figuring out what his concern is."

"So how would we have solved the problem?" asked the mother.

"I don't know how you would have ultimately solved the problem, but I'm betting there are lots of possibilities. Of course, we don't uncover those possibilities unless we're using Plan B."

As you now know, the Define the Problem step involves entering your concern or perspective into consideration. And, as you read in the last chapter, many adults enter a solution into consideration rather than a concern, causing Plan B to morph into Plan A. Let's see what that looks like:

A ten-year-old boy named Kyle went to summer camp for two months. The family therapist anticipated that Kyle and his parents would be happier than usual when they came in for their first session after he came home from camp because they wouldn't have seen one another for two *months. But it was three livid people who walked into the office.*

"What's up?" the therapist asked no one in particular once the three were seated in the office.

"They won't give me my money," the boy seethed.

"What money?" asked the therapist.

"They put two months of allowance into the camp canteen so I'd have money to spend at camp," Kyle growled. "I didn't spend all of the money they put into the canteen. NOW I WANT MY MONEY BACK!"

This sounded like a pretty specific concern, so the therapist turned to the father and asked, "What do you think?"

"Over my dead body," replied the father.

Quickly concluding that the father was using Plan A, the therapist tried to help him articulate his concern more specifically.

"What's your concern about that?"

"My concern is that Kyle's not getting his money back!"

Kaboom. The next ten minutes were fairly unpleasant. The therapist was finally able to convince the boy to leave the office, whereupon she looked at the father and asked a very important question. "I'm assuming you meant to be using Plan A, yes?"

"What makes you think that?" the father responded, a little puzzled.

"Well, if you had been using Plan B, you would have tried to work toward a mutually satisfactory solution, and if you were trying to use Plan C, you would have just given him the money," the therapist said. "You said 'Over my dead body,' which sounded very much like a 'no' to me."

"Oh, I don't care if he gets the money," the father replied.

"So what's your concern?" asked the therapist.

"My concern? What do you mean, my concern?"

"Your concern—you know, whatever's making you say 'Over my dead body.' "

"I don't like the tone he was using," said the father.

"Does Kyle know that's your concern?" the therapist asked.

"I don't know," said the father. "Why?"

"Because if your concern isn't on the table or if it's not specific enough, Kyle will have no idea what problem you guys are trying to solve, and neither will you."

Many adults manage to get through the first two steps of Plan B, but then skip the Invitation step and impose a solution anyway, thereby precipitating an explosion. Sometimes this is because the adults still can't fathom that a child might be able to collaborate on a realistic and mutually satisfactory solution. Most often, it's just a bad habit.

The mother of a nine-year-old boy named Chuck arrived at the therapist's office for an appointment one April day and was quite exasperated.

"What's up?" the therapist asked.

"He just exploded in the car," she responded.

"Over what?"

"He wants caps for his cap gun. Can you imagine? An explosion over caps?"

"I can imagine," the therapist said. "Why did he explode over caps?"

"He wants them today. I don't have time to buy them today."

"So you don't object to his having caps for his cap gun?"

"No, he can have all the caps he wants," the mother said. "I even tried to work things out with him!"

"Really? What was the solution?" the therapist asked expectantly.

"I told him I'd buy him the caps in June."

"June?"

"June," confirmed the mother. "I told him he could have the caps in June."

"How did you come up with June?"

The mother looked pleased with herself. "I don't know— it just came to me."

"Umm, I think you may have skipped a step," the therapist said.

"What do you mean?" the mother asked.

"Well, you did get two concerns onto the table—he wants caps, preferably today, and you don't have time to buy them today—but you never really invited him to solve the problem collaboratively."

"What would a good solution have been?" the mother asked.

"That's for you and Chuck to decide," the therapist said. "Something realistic and mutually satisfactory. Chuck's reaction tells us your solution wasn't mutually satisfactory."

"You really think he can do this?" said the mother.

"I've seen him do it before," said the therapist. *"But let's get Chuck in here and see."*

Chuck came into the office. *"I understand you want caps for your cap gun,"* the therapist said.

"Yeah, but she won't get them for me till June," Chuck groused.

"How come you need caps for your cap gun today?"

"Because my mom reminded me that my cousin is coming to visit in a few months, and me and him like to play with our cap guns."

"I think your mom might be willing to work on a solution to that problem with you," the therapist said.

"That was the solution!" Chuck complained.

"No, I think your mom might really be willing to work it out," the therapist said. *"Chuck, you want to buy caps—so you can play with your cap guns when your cousin comes to visit in a few months—and your mom doesn't have time to buy them for you today. Can you think of a way to work that out?"*

Chuck pondered the possibilities very briefly but then became a little agitated. *"I can't think of a way to work it out!"*

"If you need my help figuring it out, I'm happy to assist," the therapist said. *"Can you think of any ideas?"*

"NO!" Chuck screamed. *"How 'bout May?"* he pleaded in desperation.

"May could be a very good solution," said the therapist. Chuck quickly calmed. Then, knowing full well what his response would be, the therapist asked, *"When in May?"*

Without missing a beat, Chuck said, *"May first."*

The therapist looked at the mother. "How would May first be for you?"

The mother pulled out her date book, leafed through to May first, and said, "May first would be a fine day to buy caps."

The Empathy step never got rolling because your kid responded to your initial inquiry with "I don't know."

This causes many people to get stuck in the Plan B mud. To get unstuck, you'll need to figure out what kind of an "I don't know" it is.

"I don't know" can mean many different things, and the meaning of your kid's "I don't know" will, of course, determine your response. It's possible *he really doesn't know* what his concern is about the problem you're trying to discuss. It's possible he's never given the matter any thought because you've never inquired in this manner before. Proactive Plan B provides him with the opportunity to give the matter some thought. That is, if you're able to give him the chance. As you read in chapter 6, a lot of adults aren't comfortable with the silence that can occur as a kid is thinking about his concern. Remember, if you're talking while your kid is trying to think, you'll greatly reduce your chances of gathering information about your kid's concern, and thereby greatly reduce the likelihood that his concern will be addressed.

If, after you've given your kid the chance to think, you become convinced that he really has no idea what his concern is on the unsolved problem you've raised, your best option is *educated guessing*, or what might be called *hypothesis testing*. Suggest a few possibilities, based on experience, and see if any resonate. The good news is that for each problem there are finite possibilities. For example, while it might feel as though there is a universe of possible concerns interfering with your kid's completing his homework, there are probably only four or five. There are probably only four or five possible concerns for each of the other problems you and your kid are trying to solve together, too. Here's an example of educated guessing:

Adult: I've noticed that you haven't been too enthusiastic about taking your medicine. What's up?

Kid: I don't know.

Adult: Well, let's think about it. There's no rush.

Kid, after ten seconds: I really don't know.

Adult: Take your time. Let's see if we can figure it out.

Kid, after another five seconds: I really don't know.

Adult: Okay. You know we've run into this problem a few times before. Should we think about what it's been before?

Kid: I can't remember.

Adult: Well, sometimes it looks like you're having trouble swallowing the pill. Is that it?

Kid: No.

Adult: Well, sometimes it makes you sick to your stomach. Is that the problem now?

Kid: Um, no.

Adult: Does it bother you that you have to take it at
     school and the other kids see you going down to
     the nurse?

Kid: Yes!

Adult: Ah, so that's it. Anything else that we're not
     thinking of?

Kid: I don't think so.

The kid's concern is now on the table. As you're in the
midst of hypothesizing, bear in mind that your goal is to
avoid becoming a "genius," which occurs when hypothesizing turns into telling. Here's what that looks like:

Adult: I've noticed that you haven't been too
     enthusiastic about taking your medicine. What's up?

Kid: I don't know.

Adult: Well, let's think about it. There's no rush.

Kid, after ten seconds: I really don't know.

Adult: Take your time. Let's see if we can figure it out.

Kid, after another five seconds: I really don't know.

Adult: Okay. You know we've run into this problem a
     few times before. Should we think about what it's
     been before?

Kid: I can't remember.

Adult: Well, sometimes it looks like you're having
     trouble swallowing the pill. Is that it?

Kid: No.

Adult: Well, then it must be because it's making you
     sick to your stomach. So I think we need to start
     having you take it with food again.

Hmm. Promising beginning. But double-genius on the finish.

What else could "I don't know" mean? It could mean that your kid forgot or didn't understand what you asked, and if he doesn't verbalize one of those things, his facial expression will likely provide some hints. You can always inquire: "Do you remember my question?" or "Do you understand what I'm asking?" Repeat or clarify the question if necessary.

"I don't know" can also be a sign that your kid doesn't feel comfortable telling you his concern. He may be accustomed to having his concerns ignored and doesn't see the point in expressing them. He may be concerned that if he's honest, it'll cause a fight. He may need some reassurance from you that those things won't happen. Here are some ways to reassure him and encourage communication:

I'm not saying no (because you're not . . . of course, you're not saying yes either).

I'm not saying you can't (because you're not . . . then again, you're not saying he can).

I'm not saying you must (because you're not).

I'm not mad (you're not).

You're not in trouble (he's not).

I'm not telling you what to do (you're not).

I'm just trying to understand (indeed, you are).

Finally, "I don't know" can mean that your kid doesn't have the communication skills to tell you his concerns. This problem is discussed extensively in chapter 9. If you feel this might be the case, you might want to ask the following question: "Do you not know what your concern is, or do you know but are having difficulty finding the words to say?"

Incidentally, my experience is that "I don't care" doesn't mean that a kid really doesn't care. I usually assume that "I don't care" is just a variant of "I don't know." There may be instances where a kid has had so much Plan A in his life—in other words, so much of adults not caring about his concerns—that he's simply thrown in the towel on having his concerns addressed. Some reassurance that you would very much like to hear his concerns should help, eventually.

You got stuck in the Empathy step because you had trouble drilling.

It's not always easy to know what to say to keep your kid talking so you can get the information you're seeking, and there are some things kids say in response to "What's up?" that can be especially vexing. Some examples:

Adult: I've noticed we've been struggling a lot on your homework lately. What's up?

Kid: It's boring.

Adult, trying to drill a little: What's boring about it?

Kid: It's just boring.

Adult, still trying to drill: Well, can you tell me some
of the assignments that you're finding boring?
Kid: My mind is a complete blank.

Adult: I've noticed you haven't been eating what
I've been making for dinner lately. What's up?
Kid: I don't like it.
Adult, trying to drill: What don't you like about it?
Kid: It doesn't taste good.
Adult, still trying to drill: Well, can you tell me what
doesn't taste good?
Kid: It just doesn't taste good.

When initial attempts at drilling don't strike oil, you
may be inclined to abandon the well. Hang in there. You
always have educated guessing or hypothesis testing as
an option on which to fall back. But some "drilling perseverance" might be in order, too. You're looking for
some way to find out what's going on in your kid's head—
what he's thinking—and this may involve asking for details (especially on the who, what, where, and when of
the problem), comparing and contrasting, or helping
your kid imagine being "back in the moment." Let's see
what these strategies might look like. These dialogues
don't take you all the way through Plan B; they focus
solely on "drilling perseverance."

Adult: I've noticed we've been struggling a lot on
your homework lately. What's up?
Kid: It's boring.

Adult, trying to drill a little: What's boring about it?

Kid: It's just boring.

Adult, still trying to drill: Well, can you tell me some of the assignments that you're finding boring?

Kid: My mind is a complete blank.

Adult, not abandoning the well and trying to help the kid get back into the moment: Your mind is never a complete blank! Try to think of when you're sitting there trying to do homework. What are you thinking?

Kid: I'm thinking it's boring.

Adult: What else are you thinking?

Kid: I'm thinking I don't understand it. *[Voilà!]*

Adult, now asking for additional details: Is there a certain part you're thinking you don't understand?

Kid: The math. I just don't get it.

Way to hang in there! Let's try another:

Adult: I've noticed you haven't been eating what I've been making for dinner lately. What's up?

Kid: I don't like it.

Adult, trying to drill: What don't you like about it?

Kid: It doesn't taste good.

Adult, still trying to drill: Well, can you tell me what doesn't taste good?

Kid: It just doesn't taste good.

Adult not abandoning the well, comparing and contrasting: You know, I noticed that some nights

you eat what I make and some nights you don't.
Are there some things I make that you like and
some things I make that you don't?

Kid: I like pasta. (*Yesssss!*)

Adult: Yes, you do like pasta. I've noticed. But I've
noticed there are other things I make that you'll
eat.

Kid: Like what?

Adult: Rice.

Kid: Oh, yeah, rice. But when you put all that stuff in
it, like nuts, and those little slices of orange, it's
disgusting.

Adult: Anything else I make that you like?

Kid: No.

Adult, asking for additional details: Anything I make
that you especially don't like? I mean, besides
the rice with the nuts and mandarin oranges in it.

Kid: Meat. Well, I kinda like your meatballs, but that's
it. And I don't like the vegetables . . . except corn
on the cob.

Adult: I'm glad we're figuring out what you like and
don't like. That'll help us solve this problem.

Your kid stated his concern, but you didn't believe him.

While it's conceivable that your kid's first stab at identifying and articulating his concern may not be spot-on,
a lot of adults worry that the concern their kid is articulating is "wrong." If you're truly invested in understanding your kid's concern, the last thing you'd want to do is

dismiss what he tells you because you think his concern is half-baked. There are basically two options when you think your kid's concern is "wrong": (1) take his concern seriously and come up with a solution to address it, in which case you're back to Plan B when the solution doesn't solve the problem because his concern wasn't quite on target, or (2) don't take his concern seriously and let him know you think it's half-baked, in which case you've heightened the likelihood of an explosion in the moment and made it far more difficult to use Plan B the next time because you've reduced the likelihood that your kid will talk to you. I think the first option is preferable.

Your kid said he didn't care about your concern, so the air went out of your Plan B balloon.

Well, he gets ten points for honesty. Don't be insulted that he doesn't care about your concern. Let's face it, you may not actually care that much about his. The good news is that he doesn't really have to *care* about your concern; he just has to take it into account as you pursue a mutually satisfactory solution together. He'll start trying to take into account and address your concerns not too long after you take into account and start trying to address his. Here's an example:

Parent: Hector, I've noticed that we've been fighting a lot when I try to get you to come in for dinner when you're playing outside. What's up?

Hector: You always make me come in when I'm in the middle of something fun.

Parent: Yes, I was thinking that's what it was. Is there anything else about my calling you in for dinner that's hard for you?

Hector: No. I just don't want to come in if I'm in the middle of a fun game.

Parent: I understand. The thing is, you're almost always in the middle of something fun when I call you in for dinner, and it's really important to me that we eat dinner together as a family.

Hector: I don't care if we eat dinner together as a family.

Parent: Um . . . okay. Well, I guess it's probably more important to me that we eat together than it is to you. But I'm thinking that if we could get the problem solved in a way that works for both of us, then we could get it solved once and for all and then we wouldn't keep fighting about it.

Your kid didn't have any ideas for solutions.

Hopefully you did. Remember, it's not his job to solve the problem; it's the job of the Problem-Solving Team (you and him). So if your kid truly has no ideas, it's fine for you to offer some proposals, so long as you don't become a "genius" in the process. Considering solutions requires the same perseverance as drilling for concerns. This is discussed further in chapter 9.

Plan B never got off the ground because your kid blew up the minute you started talking or was too hyperactive to sit still for the conversation.

If a kid starts exploding the instant you try to initiate Proactive Plan B, many of the factors discussed in this chapter could be coming into play, and many of the remedies I've described may help. Of course, there are other possible factors that could interfere with the successful implementation of Plan B. For example, it's possible that your child lacks some language-processing skills crucial for participating in Plan B. That topic is covered in chapter 9. But there are some kids whose fuses are so short . . . who are so irritable and unhappy . . . that it's worth considering whether medication might provide some relief and make problem solving more feasible. Other kids are so hyperactive that it's hard for them to sit still long enough to participate in Plan B. Sometimes this, too, is a sign that a kid could benefit from medication. I'm very conservative about medicating kids, so I always encourage people to hang in there with Plan B before leaping to medication. But I also know that there are some kids who won't be able to participate in Plan B without the aid of medication. This topic is discussed more fully in chapter 9 as well.

Q&A

Question: If I'm using Plan B, how will my child be held accountable—you know, take responsibility—for his actions?

Answer: For too many people, the phrases "hold the child accountable" and "make him take responsibility" are really codes for "punishment." And many people believe that if the punishments a child has already received for his explosions haven't caused him to stop exploding, it must be because the punishments didn't cause the child enough pain. So they add more pain. In my experience, explosive kids have had more pain than most people experience in a lifetime. If pain were going to work, it would have worked a long time ago. The notion that the only thing these kids need is a good kick in the butt is simply wrong and doesn't do justice to the mechanisms that underlie explosive episodes. If a kid is getting his concerns on the table, taking yours into account, and working collaboratively toward a solution that works for both of you so his explosions are reduced, rest assured: he's being held accountable and taking responsibility for his actions.

Question: So I can still set limits?

Answer: Absolutely. But let's think about what you mean. "Setting limits" means you have a concern and you want to make sure it gets addressed. There are two ways to set limits: Plan A and Plan B. When you set limits using Plan A, you're increasing the likelihood of challenging behavior, solving no problems durably, teaching no skills, and slamming the door on understanding and addressing your kid's concerns. When you set limits using Plan B, you're decreasing the likelihood of challenging behavior, solving problems durably, teaching skills, and understanding and addressing your kid's concerns. Since you're probably reading this book because Plan A hasn't been getting the job done, I think Plan B is your preferred option for setting limits. The hard part is becoming good at it.

Question: Does Plan B make it clear to my child that I disapprove of his behavior?

Answer: Yes, the mere fact that you're talking to your child about his behavior is a clear sign that you disapprove of his actions. But he'll be crystal clear about your disapproval when you put your concern on the table in the Define the Problem step. It's also worth pointing out that a lot of the behavior you disapprove of occurs in the context of using Plan A. If you're not relying on Plan A and are proactively solving problems with Plan B, a lot of the challenging behavior that accompanies your child's reaction to Plan A should fade away as well.

Question: What about the real world? What if my kid has a "Plan A" boss someday?

Answer: A Plan A boss is a problem to be solved. How does your child learn to solve problems? Plan B. Which skill set is more important for life in the real world: the blind adherence to authority taught with Plan A or identifying and articulating one's concerns, taking others' concerns into account, and working toward solutions that are realistic and mutually satisfactory, which are taught with Plan B? The latter. If kids are completely dependent on imposition of adult will to do the right thing, then what will they do when adults aren't around to impose their will?

Question: Aren't safety issues best addressed with Plan A?
Answer: It depends. As described earlier in this chapter, if you're faced with an emergent safety issue, neither Plan C nor Emergency Plan B is likely to be a great option. But if your child is exhibiting predictable unsafe behavior, then Plan B may be your best long-term option for solving the problems giving rise to that behavior. Let's see what that sounds like:

Parent, initiating the Empathy step: Chris, I've noticed that it's a little hard for you to stay next to me when we're in parking lots. What's up?

Chris: I don't know.

Parent: Well, let's think about it a second. What's so hard about staying next to me when we're in the parking lot?

Chris: Um . . . I guess I'm just really excited about getting into the store.

Parent: Yes, I've noticed that you're very excited about getting into the store. Is there any other reason you think it's hard to stay next to me?

Chris: Um . . . I don't like it when you hold my hand. That's for babies.

Parent: Ah, yes, I've noticed that, too. Anything else you can think of that would help me understand why you're having trouble staying next to me in the parking lot?

Chris: Not really.

Parent: Okay. So you're having trouble staying next to me because you're really excited to get into the store and you don't like it when I hold your hand. Yes?

Chris: Uh-huh.

Parent, initiating the Define the Problem step: I understand. My concern is that it's dangerous for you to run in front of cars, and that's what happens if I don't hold your hand. And if I see that you're about to run in front of a car, I have to grab you so you don't get hurt, and then we get mad at each other. Know what I mean?

Chris: Yup.

Parent, initiating the Invitation: I wonder if there's a way for us to keep you from running in front of cars in the parking lot so you don't get hurt without me holding your hand. Do you have any ideas?

Chris: Um . . . we could not go into parking lots.

Parent: There's an idea. The thing is, sometimes we have to go into parking lots, like to go food shopping or to the drugstore. So I don't know if we can stay away from parking lots completely.

But I bet there's some way we could be in parking lots without my having to worry about you running in front of cars and without me holding your hand. What do you think?

Chris: You could leave me home with Grammy.

Parent: I could, sometimes. But Grammy can't always look after you when I'm out doing errands.

Chris: I could hold your belt loop.

Parent: You could hold my belt loop. That would be better than me holding your hand?

Chris: Yes. Holding hands is for babies.

Parent: You'd hold my belt loop even if you were really excited about getting into the store?

Chris: Yes.

Parent: What if I'm wearing something that doesn't have a belt loop?

Chris: Um . . . I guess I could just hold onto whatever you're wearing.

Parent: I think that idea could work very well. Can I remind you to hold my belt loop before we get out of the car?

Chris: Yes.

Parent: But sometimes you get mad when I remind you.

Chris: I only get mad if you're screaming at me to hold your hand.

Parent: I'm screaming at you because you're— um—you know what? If you and I agree that you're going to hold my belt loop in the parking

lot from now on, then it won't matter why I was
screaming at you.

Chris: What if you forget not to scream at me?

Parent: I'm going to try very hard not to. If I slip, can
you remind me?

Chris: Yup.

Parent: This plan work for you?

Chris: Yup.

Parent: It works for me, too. And if our solution
doesn't work, we'll talk about it some more and
think of another solution.

Once again, when parents say "safety issues,"
they're frequently referring to what their child is
doing in the midst of an explosion (hitting, throwing
things, etc.). But since most explosions are precipitated by an adult using Plan A, the antidote is to use
Plan B instead of Plan A.

Question: What should I do if my child explodes?

Answer: If your child is exploding, it's a pretty sure bet
you're using Plan A. If you're lucky and your child is
still, at that moment, capable of rational thought, then
Emergency Plan B is an option. If not, then one viable
option is to use Plan C at that moment and use Proactive Plan B during your next opportunity to solve the
problem that caused him to explode in the first place.
But if you have to endure an explosion, don't let it go
to waste. Explosions provide very important information about unsolved problems you may have missed or

failed to prioritize. But that's the only productive thing about explosions: they let you know there's a need for Proactive Plan B so you can prevent another explosion over the same problem the next time.

Question: I don't have time to use Plan B. It takes too long.

Answer: You don't have time not to use Plan B! Explosions always take longer to deal with than Plan B would have taken to prevent them. Unsolved problems always take more time than solved problems. Doing something that isn't working always takes more time than doing something that will work. And if you're doing a lot of Proactive Plan B—solving problems with durable solutions—then the amount of time you're spending using Plan B will decrease as problems are solved.

Question: I'm not that quick on my feet. I can't always decide what Plan to use on the spur of the moment.

Answer: All the more reason for you to be solving problems proactively rather than emergently. It's only with Emergency Plan B that you have to be quick on your feet. If you find yourself in an emergent situation and you can't decide what Plan to use, your default option is Plan B.

Question: I started using Plan B with my daughter, and she talked! In fact, she talked so much and I gathered so much information that I started becoming over-whelmed with all the problems we need to solve! Help!

Answer: It's true, sometimes Plan B opens the information floodgates, and it can feel like Plan B is about to topple over under the weight of so many unsolved problems. Your goal is to sort through and perhaps make a list of all the problems—you probably won't make it past the Empathy step in doing this—and then start solving one problem at a time. Your daughter would probably be delighted to help with the prioritizing.

Question: So I'm not a failure if I don't make it through all three steps of Plan B in one sitting?

Answer: Not at all. If you didn't make it past the Empathy step in the first attempt at Plan B on a given problem, but you now understand your kid's concerns on that problem, I'd say you've been quite successful! Just make sure you follow up with the next two steps before too much time passes.

Question: What if my child and I agree on a solution and then he won't do what he agreed to?

Answer: As you'll read in chapter 9, that's usually a sign that the solution wasn't as realistic and mutually satisfactory as you may first have thought. That's not a catastrophe, just a reminder that the first solution to a problem often doesn't get the job done. Remember, good solutions are usually variants of the solutions that preceded them. It's also important to remember that Plan B isn't an exercise in wishful thinking. Both parties need to be able to follow through on their part of the solution. If your child isn't following through, it's probably not because he won't but because he can't. Work toward a solution that he can actually do. By the way, kids aren't the only ones who don't follow through on what they've agreed to; sometimes adults have a similar tendency.

Question: I did it! My child and I did Plan B together and we solved our first problem. Well, the solution seems to be working so far. Now what?

Answer: Well done! And good for you for realizing that the solution may not stand the test of time. You're on your way to having the problem durably solved, though. What's next? Move on to another unsolved problem. And then another. Along the way, be sure to take a step back to notice the progress you're making.

8

B Scenes

You've already been provided quite a bit of information: a key theme (*kids do well if they can*); what you're working on (unsolved problems and lagging skills); why enforcing consequences often doesn't get the job done (and can, in fact, make things worse); the three Plans (one in particular); the different ways in which Plan B can go awry (and how to get back on track). A lot of people tell me that they had to read chapters 6 and 7 several times before the content settled in.

People also tell me that they need lots of examples so they can get a better feel for the language of Plan B on a wide variety of unsolved problems. And while there are lots of examples throughout this book, the purpose of this chapter is to provide you with some one-stop shopping. Mind you, there is no Plan B "script," so even if you're trying to solve some of the same problems with your kid as those depicted in this chapter, your Plan B is almost certain to take different twists and turns. This chapter also provides us with an opportunity to reacquaint ourselves with some of the kids you met in chapter 4.

Let's start with what we might call "seamless" Proactive Plan B, just to provide an example of what it looks like when nothing goes wrong:

Father: I've noticed it's been a little hard for you to sleep in your own bed lately. What's up?

Child: I'm scared.

Father: What are you scared about?

Child: I'm scared of robbers.

Father: Robbers?

Child: Yes, but only at night.

Father: So, you're not scared of robbers during the day.

Child: No, only when I'm lying in bed at night.

Father: What are you worried a robber would do?

Child: I don't know what a robber would do. I just know it scares me to think of someone getting into our house.

Father: What's the scary part of it for you? What would you see happening?

Child: Seeing someone grinning at me with, like, this evil grin.

Father: Ah, that is scary. And I think I'm sorry I let you watch that Harry Potter movie.

Child: Yeah, that wasn't a very good idea.

Father: Well, I think I understand why you're scared of robbers. The thing is, when you get scared of robbers at night, you come into our bed. And then two things happen. I wake up and can't fall back asleep. And Mommy has to leave and sleep in your bed because it gets too crowded in ours.

Child: She doesn't have to leave.

Father: Well, she has trouble sleeping in the bed when it's too crowded. So I'm wondering if there's a way to help you with being scared of robbers at night . . . without me getting woken up and Mommy having to leave.

Child: I could come into your bed really quietly.

Father: Yes, you could try being even quieter. I think what wakes me up is when you crawl over me to get in the middle.

Child: I could crawl over Mommy. She doesn't have any trouble falling back asleep.

Father: Yes, that could work. Although, that solution still wouldn't take care of Mommy being too crowded and leaving.

Child: Oh, yeah.

[Silence.]

Father: Do you have any other ideas?

Child: No.

Father: I have one. Should we see what you think of it?

Child: Okay.

Father: I was thinking we could make you a little bed right next to our bed . . . then you could feel safe because you'd be with us, but you wouldn't wake me up when you get in and wouldn't make Mommy feel too crowded.

Child: I don't know if that would make me feel safe enough.

Father: What do you mean?

Child: I don't know if lying in a bed next to you would make me feel as safe as lying right next to you.

Father: Well, think about it a little.

Child: I guess we could try it. But I don't know if it'll work.

Father: Well, we could do that. Or we could try to think of some other ideas now.

Child: We could try your idea.

Father: Okay. Let's give it a try and then, if it doesn't work, we'll try to think of some other ideas. Thanks for talking about this with me, buddy.

Child: Okay.

Sometimes Plan B goes that smoothly. Often it doesn't. While "seamless" Plan B may be faster, speed is not necessarily the goal. Some unsolved problems are more complicated and take longer. Plan B comes more

naturally to some kids and adults than others. So don't
be dismayed if Plan B doesn't proceed as smoothly as you
might have hoped.

You may recall that Danny, from chapter 4, often
became upset when he was being nagged by his mother,
but we were lacking details on the specific problems she
was nagging him about. It turns out that one of those
problems was screen time. Here's her first attempt at
Proactive Plan B:

Mother: Danny, I've noticed that we've been
fighting a lot about how much time you're
spending in front of the screen after school. Is
that something we could talk about?

Danny: No.

Mother: When would be a good time for us to talk
about that?

Danny: Never.

Mother: Never is an awfully long time for us to keep
fighting about this problem. Isn't there a time we
could talk about it so we could finally stop
fighting about it?

Danny: Are you going to keep bugging me until I
talk about it?

Mother: Actually, I was hoping if we talked about it I
could bug you less, since it's one of the things I
bug you about the most.

Danny: Fine, talk.

Mother: Well, I'm hoping you'll talk, too. I just wanted to get your take on why we're fighting about it so much.

Danny: Because you won't stop bugging me about it, that's why.

Mother: Okay, I understand that you'd like me to bug you less. But I'm bugging you about it because you'll watch TV or play your computer games for a very long time if I don't.

Danny: Well, I don't have anything else to do.

Mother, slipping into advice-giving: Sure you do! You could read, or you could ride your bike. . .

Danny, with his typical response to his mother's advice-giving: I don't want to do any of that stuff! See, I knew talking about this was a waste of time!

Mother: Hmm. I guess you didn't want to hear about the things I thought you could do instead.

Danny: Duh.

Mother: So let's get back to what we were talking about. You were saying that you don't have anything else to do.

Danny: I don't! I would shoot hoops, or play street hockey, but I don't have anyone to play with. And it's boring to do that stuff by myself. So I just play video games or watch TV.

Mother: If you had kids to play with after school, you wouldn't spend so much time in front of the screen?

Danny: Yes.

Mother: Is there anything else I should know about why you're spending so much time in front of the screen?

Danny: I like it.

Mother: You like it?

Danny: It's relaxing. I work really hard in school and I want to relax a little before I have to spend two hours on homework.

Mother: Okay. So, you like your TV and video games and you don't have anyone to play with. Yes?

Danny: Yes.

Mother: So, my concern is that you're spending two or three hours in front of the screen everyday. And that's a ton of screen time.

Danny: I know a lot of kids who spend that much time in front of the screen. Matt's parents let him play whenever he wants.

Mother: Hmm. Well, I don't know Matt's parents very well. Maybe they aren't worried about their kid staring at a screen for three or fours hours a day. But I am. I'm not saying you shouldn't have any screen time. I'm just thinking that three hours is a lot of time in front of a screen. So, I wonder if there's a way for us to make sure you still have screen time . . . because it relaxes you . . . but also see if we can find a way for you to have kids to do things with after school so you're not spending the entire afternoon in front of a screen. Do you have any ideas?

Danny: No.

Mother: Well, let's think about it. We've never really talked about this problem like this before.

Danny: I can't think of anything. And I don't want to talk about it anymore.

Mother: I don't know if I have any ideas at the moment either. But let's think about it. We're in no rush.

Danny: I can't talk about it anymore! I can't think of anything!

Mother: Maybe we should both think about it a little—not now, though—and then talk about it some more another time. Just because we can't come up with any ideas now doesn't mean there aren't any ideas.

Danny: Well, I don't have any.

Mother: So, let's stop talking now and come back to it. When should we do that?

Danny: I don't know!

Mother: How 'bout I ask you later. I think you're pretty talked out right now.

Danny: Fine!

At bedtime that night, Plan B resumed. Sort of:

Mother: Danny, would this be a good time to continue our conversation?

Danny: What conversation?

Mother: The conversation we were having about screen time.

Danny: I don't want to talk about that right now! I'm too tired! And I didn't think of any ideas anyway.

Mother: Okay. We don't have to talk about it now. I did think of an idea, but I think you may be too tired to hear about it.

Danny: I am.

Mother: Okay, let's try again tomorrow.

The next day, at dinnertime:

Danny: Can I hear your idea about screen time?

Mother: My idea? Oh, uh, sure. You know, I was thinking that there's a sports program at the Y after school three days a week. Justin's mom told me about it because he goes. They play all kinds of sports. I thought maybe you could do that and then you'd have kids to play sports with. What do you think?

Danny: I'm not very good friends with Justin.

Mother: Okay.

Danny: And what if they play a sport I don't like?

Mother: I don't know that much about it. But I think you get to choose the sports you want to play.

Danny: What if I don't like it?

Mother: Well, we really don't know anything about it yet. I was just thinking we could check it out. If you want to.

Danny: Do you know what sports they have?

Mother: Not really. I really don't know anything about it. It was just an idea.

Danny: I don't know. . .

Mother: Well, think about it. It's not like you're signing up if you're just thinking about it. And if you decide you want to see what it's like, we could go over there one day. If I can get off from work early. Maybe I should call Justin's mother and she can tell us about it. What do you think?

Danny: Okay.

Is this problem solved yet? No. Has the conversation started? Yes. Did Danny's mother make it through all three steps in the first try? No. Did she patiently come back to the problem at a later time? Yes. Is Danny participating? Yes. Thinking? A little. Not done, but better.

But let's move on to one final example of Proactive Plan B. My goal in this dialogue is to demonstrate just how complicated some problems can become. Hang in there with Plan B. The problem won't get solved with Plan A or Plan C.

Mother: So, we set up this time to talk about our amusement park problem. Where should we begin?

Jordan: How about with how unfair you are.

Father: Ah, this is going to be fun.

Mother: How am I unfair?

Jordan: You're taking Lucy to the amusement park with a friend, and you won't let me take a friend. That's not fair.

Mother: Tell me how that's not fair. I do lots of things with you without Lucy tagging along.

Jordan: It's not fair because I haven't seen my friend Cassie for three weeks, and I missed her birthday party because you guys made me go on that stupid camping trip, which I hated! And I want to do something special with her this Saturday because I haven't seen her in three weeks, and I don't want to do something boring with her, and the amusement park would be so much fun for us!

Mother: I understand that you want to do something really fun with Cassie. You can't think of anything else Cassie and you could do together that would be fun besides coming to the amusement park?

Jordan: No!

Mother: The lake?

Jordan: Boring.

Mother: The movies?

Jordan: Come on!

Mother: Okay, well, here's my concern about the amusement park. The reason I want to take your sister and her friend—alone—is because you and your sister fight nonstop, and I really don't want the fighting to ruin her day or embarrass her in front of her friend. This is supposed to be a fun day for her.

Jordan: I wouldn't fight with her! I wouldn't even be around her. I promise!

Mother: You and Cassie would do your own thing at the amusement part and leave Lucy and her friend alone?

Jordan: Yes! I don't want to be with Lucy and her friend!

Father: I can't imagine you and Lucy being in the car together and not fighting.

Jordan: Stop! We wouldn't fight in the car!

Father: You guys always fight in the car.

Mother: And my concern is that I really don't want to take that chance. This is supposed to be Lucy's special day, and I don't want it to get ruined. So that's the problem we're trying to solve. You want to have a really fun day with your friend, and you feel the amusement park . . . on Saturday . . . is the only way to do that, and I want to make sure your sister has a special day with her friend without fighting with you. Can you think of any way for us to work that out?

Jordan: Dad could drive me and Cassie to the amusement park. Then you wouldn't have to worry about me and Lucy fighting in the car, and I would promise to stay away from her and her friend while we're at the park.

Father: No way.

Jordan: Why not!

Father: Because the amusement park is an hour away, and driving you and your friend to the amusement park is not what I had planned for Saturday.

Jordan: What's the big deal? You wouldn't have to stay! Come on!

Father: If I don't stay, then I'm driving two hours back and forth at the beginning of the day and two hours back and forth at the end of the day. That's a big chunk of my day, and I have a lot of things to do on Saturday. I'm not doing it.

Jordan: This is so unfair!

Father: No, you're being unfair! This always happens! You guys have a problem and it's Dad to the rescue! Well, I'm tired of being the rescue squad. Plus, even if I was willing to drive you, I'm not paying for you and your friend to go to the amusement park. This is Lucy's birthday present, but the only reason you want to go to the amusement park is because you can't think of anything else to do.

Jordan: I would pay for it myself! And Cassie would pay for herself!

Father: Why does it have to be Saturday? Why can't you and Cassie go a different day when I don't have other things I need to do?

Jordan (starting to cry): Because we were planning on seeing each other Saturday, and I haven't seen her in three weeks, and I want to do something really fun with her.

Father: Well, I still need to think about whether I'm willing to drive you. Plus, if you and your sister are at the amusement park with friends, then your brother's going to want to bring a friend to the amusement park, and then my day is completely shot.

Mother: Robbie's spending the day at my mother's on Saturday.

Father: Oh.

Mother, to husband: So, I guess you have to decide if you're willing to drive Jordan and Cassie to the amusement park and back on Saturday.

Jordan: This is so unfair!

Mother: Could you stop saying it's unfair? We're sitting here trying to solve this problem so it works for everyone. That's not unfair!

Jordan: Maybe Cassie's mom could drive one way.

Mother: You mean, she could drop you off or pick you up?

Jordan: Maybe. I don't know.

Mother, to father: Are you willing to drive one way if Cassie's mom can drive the other?

Father: I'm thinking about it. But I'm not paying for Jordan and Cassie.

Jordan: I've got that part! I said we'd pay for ourselves!

Father: And you'd stay away from your sister while you're in the park?

Jordan: I don't want to be anywhere near that little brat!

Father: Nice. Well, I guess I'd be willing to drive one way. How are we finding out if Cassie's mother will drive the other way?

Jordan: I'll call her!

Father: What are we doing if she can't?
Mother: I guess we'll have to sit down and talk about it some more.

Plan B isn't always simple and it's usually not fast. But explosions take longer and don't solve anything.

While Proactive Plan B is far preferable and has been our primary focus in this chapter (and this book), there will be times—hopefully, few and far between—where you need to call on Plan B under more emergent circumstances. So here's an example of Emergency Plan B:

Mother: Mark, it's time to go to your swim lesson.
Mark, playing with Legos at the kitchen table: I'm not going. I hate swim lessons.
Mother: Mark, we have a problem, because your brother has a swim lesson, too, and I can't leave you home alone.
Mark: I don't care! I'm not going!
Mother: We need to find a way to work this out. You don't want to go to your swim lesson, but I need to take—
Mark, slamming his fist on the table, red-faced: HOW MANY TIMES DO I HAVE TO TELL YOU?! I HATE SWIMMING! I'M NOT GOING! GET AWAY FROM ME!
Mother: Mark, I didn't say you had to go to your swim lesson. I said we have to find a way to work this out. That's different.
Mark: I'm sick of working things out. IF YOU DON'T SHUT UP, I'M GOING TO KILL YOU!

James (Mark's brother): Mom, I'm gonna be late for my swim lesson!

Mother: James, can you go get my purse? I think it's in my bedroom. Mark, I'm not saying you have to go to your swim lesson. I'm just trying to think of how we can get your brother to his swim lesson without me leaving you home alone. Do you have any ideas?

Mark: No!

Mother: I might have an idea. Would you like to hear it?

Mark: Fine!

Mother: Can you take the Legos with you and you can work on your Legos while your brother is at his swim lesson?

Mark: The pieces will break apart. I don't want to go.

Mother: I understand that you don't want to go. I'm not saying you have to take your swim lesson. But I can't leave you home alone. The only way I can think of to work this out is for you to come with me and bring the Legos along. If you have a different idea, I'm happy to listen.

Mark: (*no response*)

Mother: What do you think?

James, back from retrieving the purse: I'm going to be late!

Mark, to James: SHUT UP, JERK!

James: No, you shut up!

Mother: James, please go wait for me by the front door.

James: He told me to shut up!

Mother: I heard what he told you. It wasn't very nice. Now go wait for me by the front door please.

Mother: Mark, the only way I can think of to work this out is for you to bring the Legos to your brother's swim lesson. If you can think of other solutions, I'm happy to listen.

Mark, starting to pack up his Legos: I'm not taking a swim lesson, so don't try to make me. Look! I told you the Legos were going to break apart!

Mother, switching to the new problem: Let's figure out how to transport the Legos so they don't fall apart. Thanks for trying to work this out.

Mark: I wasn't trying to work it out.

Mother: Well, you did a good job anyway.

Is the swimming lesson problem solved durably? Not yet. That problem should be the focus of Proactive Plan B as soon as possible so a more durable solution can be found.

Need another example of Emergency Plan B? Here goes. Casey and his parents and sister took a trip to Disney World, and their first day went wonderfully. They were a pretty tired,* hungry* crew as they left* the Magic Kingdom on their way back to their hotel (asterisks denote well-established vulnerabilities for Casey: fatigue, hunger, and transitions). Of course, this scenario had graver implications for Casey than for his sister. Just after they were outside the gates, Casey uttered the following ominous request: "I want cotton candy."

"You can't have cotton candy because we're not going back into the park to look for it," said the father insistently.

Casey stopped dead in his tracks. "I want cotton candy!" he said loudly.

The parents exchanged glances. They contemplated their three emergent options. Plan A would only cause a lengthy explosion. Nothing to be gained there. That left only Plan B and Plan C. Going back into the park for cotton candy would have been extremely inconvenient, and Casey had already had a healthy dose of sugar for the day. So Plan C wasn't ideal because the parents did have a concern to put on the table.

"Casey, I think you're very tired," the mother said, trying a little old-fashioned empathy.

"I want cotton candy!" he said, moving closer to the edge of the cliff.

The father tried some new-fangled empathy in an attempt to clarify Casey's concern. "You want cotton candy!" he said. "What's up?"

"I want cotton candy!" said Casey.

Maybe there was nothing to clarify, but the father tried a little drilling. "Is it because you're hungry?"

"I just want a snack and I really wanted to have some cotton candy today and I never did!"

"Okay, so you had your heart set on cotton candy and we never had any today. Yes?"

"Yes!"

"So let's think about this for a second. You really wanted cotton candy today and we never got any. And you want a snack before dinner. The thing is you've had a lot of other sugary stuff today . . . that candied apple and the soda you had with lunch. So I think Mommy and I were hoping maybe you could have a snack that wasn't so sugary. Do you have any ideas for how we could get you a snack but have it not be so sugary?"

"No!" Casey pouted, crossing his arms, still on the edge.

"Well, let's think about this for a second," said the father, crouching down next to his son. "We could just wait until we're back in the park tomorrow to buy cotton candy. And we could buy you something to snack on right now that isn't so sugary. Can you think of something else you'd like to eat on the way to the hotel besides cotton candy?"

"I want cotton candy," whined Casey, but his tone suggested that rational thought might slowly be returning.

"I know you do."

Casey started walking toward the car again.

"I wonder what else you might like to have for a snack," the father said. "I think there's a McDonald's on the way back to the hotel."

"French fries?" volunteered Casey.

"Don't forget, this is just a snack, guys," said the mother.

When the family arrived at McDonald's, Casey ordered his fries, ate them happily, and ate a reasonably healthy dinner back at the hotel.

Had the parents decided to handle the cotton candy problem with Plan A, they would likely have endured yet another long explosion. Had they decided to handle things using Plan C, they would have gone back into the park for cotton candy. By using Emergency Plan B, they averted an explosion on an important issue and were able to see the problem through to a realistic and mutually satisfactory solution. By the way, Emergency Plan B tends to go more smoothly if you and your kid have a lot of Proactive Plan B practice under your belts.

Okay, one last example of Emergency Plan B (lest you become too enthusiastic about its use). One night, Helen had somehow decided that she wanted to do her homework sitting atop the heater vent in the kitchen. Helen's father objected to her doing her homework sitting atop the vent. This minor disagreement—which had never arisen before—had the potential to totally disrupt Helen's completion of her homework by inducing a prolonged explosion.

"Helen, I don't want you to do your homework sitting on the vent," said the father.

"I want to," Helen whined.

"Helen, I want you to come over to the kitchen table and do your homework," commanded the father, now moving toward Plan A.

"I want to sit here!" Helen whined with a little more fervor.

The father caught himself. Should he continue with Plan A, just let it go with Plan C, or use Emergency Plan B? The father quickly called to mind that there was little to be gained by dismissing his daughter's concern. In fact, he didn't even know what her concern was! Nor his own! The father began the Empathy step.

"Helen, you want to sit on the vent. What's up?"

"It's warmer," she replied.

"You want to sit on the vent because it's warmer." The father now had to give serious thought to his own concern (if he really had one) and whether he wanted to put it on the table. If he decided he had no concern, of course, he would have simply chosen Plan C. "I don't want your papers scattered all over the floor. Let's see if we can work this out. I wonder if there's a way for you to be warm without your papers getting scattered all over the floor. Do you have any ideas?"

"No, I want to sit here." Helen pouted.

"Oh, there must be a way to solve this problem," he prodded. "We've had tougher problems than this before. Let's think," the father encouraged.

"How 'bout I do my homework on the vent tonight and at the kitchen table tomorrow night?" volunteered Helen.

"Well, that's an idea, but your papers would still be scattered all over the floor tonight," said the father. "Can you think of some other way for us to solve this problem?"

"No, that's it!" Helen responded.

"There has to be some way for you to not be cold and for the papers not to be scattered all over the floor," the father said. "I have some ideas. Would you like to hear them?"

"Umm . . . okay."

"We could turn up the heat so you wouldn't be cold. Or you could put on a sweater. Or we could find some way for your papers not to be scattered all over the floor. Any of those ideas work for you?"

"I think we should turn up the heat," said Helen.

"So if we turn up the heat so you won't be cold, you won't need to sit on the vent?"

"Yeah."

"Do you want me to help you move your things?"

"No, just go turn up the heat," said Helen.

"You did a very nice job of working things out," said the father.

In the next meeting with the family therapist, the father needed a little reassurance. "I'm afraid we're teaching her that she never has to listen to us, and I don't think that bodes well for the future."

"She never does what you tell her to now?" the therapist asked.

"No, she actually does what we ask quite often," the father replied. "I'm worried that she'll think that all she has to do is start to throw a fit to get what she wants."

"You've been using Plan B for a few months now. Is she exploding less or more?"

"A lot less." The father smiled.

"Do you have more unsolved problems than before or less?"

"Less."

"Are you yelling a lot less?"

"Yes."

"How are you and Helen getting along lately?"

"A lot better. You know, Helen was always a very affectionate kid. But we were battling so much that, up until a few weeks ago, when I'd get home from work, she'd barely even acknowledge my presence. For the past two weeks, when I get home from work, she jumps up from whatever she's doing and gives me a big hug."

"I think we're doing okay," the therapist said.

"But what about the real world?" the father asked.

"What about it?" the therapist asked.

"The real world doesn't have Plan B or people who always try to understand," he said.

"I don't think that fighting with her a lot will help her live in the real world. On the other hand, I do expect that helping her learn how to solve problems that come up in her life—how to think about and state her concerns, take someone else's concerns into account, and work toward mutually satisfactory and realistic solutions—is going to serve her very well in the real world."

9

Extra Help

In an ideal world, you've begun reducing your use of Plan A by now. And you've placed some unsolved problems on the back burner (Plan C) so they're not causing explosions anymore. And you've begun using Plan B to get the ball rolling on solving the problems that have been setting the stage for explosive episodes between you and your child (hopefully, the troubleshooting information in chapter 7 and examples in chapter 8 helped to smooth out some of the rough edges). So, if all of those things are true, then things should be starting to settle down a little between you and your explosive kid.

Of course—and you don't need me to tell you this—

the world of parenting an explosive kid is often far from ideal. Sometimes, kids have difficulty participating in Plan B because of factors that might be well addressed by medication. And sometimes kids have issues with communication skills that make it hard (but not impossible) for them to participate in Plan B. And you may still be wondering how working on unsolved problems helps teach kids the skills they lack. These topics are covered in this chapter.

WHEN MEDICATION CAN HELP

There are some kids who are so hyperactive, or impulsive, or distractible, or irritable, or obsessive, or have such a short fuse and are so emotionally reactive, that it's extremely difficult for them to participate in Plan B until these issues have been satisfactorily addressed. And if any of these issues are making participation in Plan B difficult, then they're presumably making other aspects of life difficult as well. These are issues for which medication can sometimes be helpful.

Many parents have an instant negative reaction to the idea of medicating their child, and for good reason. These days, too many kids are medicated unnecessarily, too many are on too much medication, and too many are on medication for things medication does not address well. Psychotropic medication isn't always prescribed with the level of care and diligence it deserves, and it's not always prescribed by people who have a sufficient level of expertise. Medication doesn't teach any lagging thinking skills or solve any problems collaboratively. But medication can help kids be more available and accessible for problems to be solved and skills to be taught. So while a conservative approach to medication is totally appropriate, you may not want to rule out the possibility completely. In some kids, medication is an indispensable component of treatment (although it's important to remember that Plan A has an excellent chance of causing explosions even when your kid is on an effective regimen of medication). My goal here is not to cover medication exhaustively but rather to review some of the more common options.

If inattention and distractibility are significantly interfering with your child's academic progress or making it difficult for him to sustain focus long enough to participate meaningfully in Plan B discussions, medication may offer some promise. The mainstays of medical treatment for inattention are the stimulant medications (for example, Ritalin, Focalin, Vyvanse, and Concerta), some of which have been in use for more than sixty years. If hyperactivity and poor impulse control are setting the stage for significant behavior problems at school, interfering with academic progress, or making it difficult for your kid to sit still long enough to participate in Plan B, stimulants are again typically the first choice. In some kids, the lack of a positive response to stimulants, side effects, or complicating conditions may warrant consideration of alternative, nonstimulant medications (for example, Strattera).

One of the more challenging aspects of using stimulant medication is that when it's effective, many parents report that they have "two different kids": the kid who's less hyperactive and impulsive and more focused (when the medication is on board) and the kid who's not (when the medication hasn't been given or has worn off). As it relates to Plan B, this means that sometimes you have a kid who's able to sit still for and focus on solving problems and sometimes you don't. It also means that when you and your kid are contemplating whether a solution is truly realistic, you must consider the conditions—i.e., with medication or without—under which the solution is typically going to be enacted. Solutions that are realistic when your child is medicated may not be so realistic when he's not.

Some kids are so irritable, cranky, grouchy, and grumpy that even the smallest bump in the road can feel insurmountable or inordinately upsetting. A class of antidepressants called selective serotonin re-uptake inhibitors (SSRIs; for example, Lexapro and Prozac) may offer some relief. Similar medications may also be helpful for some kids who are obsessive or obsessive-compulsive. Finally, if despite heavy doses of Plan B and Plan C and drastically reduced use of Plan A, your child is still so short-fused or emotionally reactive that he is incapable of participating in Plan B discussions, a class of medications called atypical antipsychotics (for example, Risperdal and Abilify) may be helpful.

Deciding whether to medicate one's child *should* be difficult; you'll need a lot of information, much more than is provided here, especially about side effects. Some medications that are commonly prescribed for kids haven't actually been approved for use with kids, nor have many been studied extensively in use with children and adolescents, especially with regard to their long-term side effects. Your doctor should help you weigh the anticipated benefits of medication with the potential risks so you can make educated decisions. Although it's important to have faith in the doctor's expertise, it's equally important that you feel comfortable with the treatment plan he or she proposes, or at least that you're comfortable with the balance between benefits and risks. If you are not comfortable with or confident in the information you've been given, you need more information. If your doctor doesn't have the time or expertise to provide you with more information, you need a new doctor. Medical treatment is not something to fear, but it needs to be implemented competently and compassionately and monitored continuously. Ultimately, what you'll need most of all is a competent, clinically savvy, attentive, and available prescribing doctor. You'll want one who:

- takes the time to get to know you and your child, listens to you, and is familiar with treatment options that have nothing to do with a prescription pad;

- knows that a diagnosis provides little useful information about your kid;

- understands that there are some things medication doesn't treat well at all;

- has a good working knowledge of the potential side effects of medication and their management;

- makes sure that you—and your kid, if it's appropriate—understand each medication and its anticipated benefits and potential side effects and interactions with other medications; and

- is willing to devote sufficient time to monitoring your child's progress carefully and continuously over time.

When children have a poor response to medication, it is often because one of the foregoing elements was missing from their treatment.

A discreet approach to medication is also recommended. A lot of kids aren't eager for their classmates to know that they're receiving medication to address emotional or behavioral issues. If there's no way to keep your child's classmates in the dark, it's often necessary to educate the classmates about individual differences (asthma, allergies, diabetes, difficulty concentrating, low frustration tolerance, etc.) that may require medicinal treatment. On the other hand, while there's a temptation for parents to avoid doing so, I typically encourage parents to keep relevant school personnel well informed about their child's medication. The observations and feedback of teachers are often crucial to making appropriate adjustments in medication, and as discussed more fully in chapter 11, the goal is to work as a collaborative team.

KIDS WHO HAVE
DIFFICULTY COMMUNICATING

If you're the parent of a child whose communication skills are significantly compromised, you may be wondering if Plan B is truly realistic for your kid. You may be wondering if it's actually going to be possible to figure out what your kid's concerns are or whether he's going to be able to participate in considering potential solutions. Since all of the examples of Plan B you've read so far depict kids with half-decent communication skills, it's no wonder you're wondering. Communication difficulties can span a broad range of issues, and many of the strategies described in chapter 7 would be useful with kids whose communication difficulties are mild. The focus here is on kids whose communication difficulties are toward the more severe end of the spectrum.

The good news is that Plan B can be adjusted for kids with compromised communication skills so that you can identify unsolved problems, gather some information about the concerns related to these unsolved problems, and participate with your kid in the process of generating and evaluating solutions. Of course, applying Plan B *proactively* is every bit as important with explosive kids who have compromised communication skills as it is with explosive kids whose communication skills are intact.

Identifying Unsolved Problems

The first challenge is to create a list of the unsolved problems that are reliably and predictably precipitating your kid's challenging episodes, and in this circumstance we may need to relax a little on a key tenet of the Empathy step to accomplish the mission. If your child doesn't have the linguistic wherewithal to participate in generating the list, your own observations about the situations in which explosions typically occur will be absolutely essential. Explosive episodes are no less predictable in kids who have compromised communication skills; it's just that they have more difficulty communicating what's causing their frustration. So . . . and it's not easy for me to say this, but here goes: in the case of these kids, it's okay for adults to be "geniuses" in generating the list of unsolved problems.

Now, how much of a genius you should be and the form the list takes depends on the severity of your child's communication skill difficulties. An adolescent boy I worked with was able to participate in some degree of linguistic give-and-take, but was unable to provide much information about the unsolved problems precipitating his explosive episodes. His parents and teachers gave thought to the conditions under which such episodes were most likely and recorded their ideas on an index card: being hot, being tired, being hungry, thinking someone was mad at him, being surprised, and having difficulty with an academic task. The parents and teachers kept their index cards handy, and whenever the boy would start to become agitated, they would recite the possibilities to him to find out which might be the cause. The adults memorized the items rather rapidly, thereby eliminating the need for the index card; the kid eventually memorized the possibilities as well. He became much better at verbalizing problems—for example, instead of exploding, he'd say, "I'm hot"—and solutions to these common problems were solved through use of Proactive Plan B.

A girl I worked with had extremely limited communication skills; grunting, crying, screaming, and hitting were the extent of her repertoire. For her, we depicted in pictures shown on a laminated card the unsolved problems that were reliably and predictably precipitating her explosive episodes. When the girl needed to let adults know there was a problem, or when she began exhibiting signs of frustration, the adults would ask her to point to the picture that best communicated what was frustrating her. As the girl pointed at a picture, the adults would verbally confirm the problem (e.g., "Ah, you're hungry") and move on to a different laminated card that depicted potential solutions corresponding to that unsolved problem (described below). Of course, every once in a while, the girl had a problem that was not already depicted in pictures and a new picture was added to the "problem card." The ultimate goal was for her to begin using actual words rather than pointing to communicate about problems, but explosions—and the need for immediate guesswork on the part of adults—were dramatically reduced through use of this fairly basic communication tool.

Perhaps this goes without saying, but when a kid has significant communication challenges or other cognitive impairments, it is crucial to give very serious consideration to the words or concepts that are of the highest priority and that need to be taught first. If you overload the kid with new words, you'll reduce the likelihood of the use of any. I recommend prioritizing words or concepts needed for pinpointing unsolved problems or concerns, solving problems, and handling frustration, because not having these words causes the kids' most challenging moments and impedes their ability to learn much else.

The CPS model doesn't place a strong emphasis on teaching kids a vocabulary for feelings. While it's useful for a kid to learn to communicate that he's sad, mad, or frustrated, it's more important for him to communicate what problems are causing him to be sad, mad, or frustrated in the first place. Otherwise, it won't be clear what problems need to be solved.

Of course, specific concerns, such as "I'm hot" only apply to situations in which a kid is hot. You may find it useful to teach a more generic "problem vocabulary" that can be applied across many situations. A variety of phrases—for example, "Something's the matter," "I can't talk about that right now," "I need help," "I don't know what to do," and "I need a break"—are applicable to a wider range of circumstances and can be taught through repetition (for example, saying "Looks like something's the matter" whenever it looks like something's the matter). Most kids only need to be taught one or two phrases most applicable to their specific requirements. We adults overestimate the linguistic skills we use to let people know we're frustrated or stuck or overwhelmed; the truth is, most adults lean on a few key phrases. By teaching a few key phrases to kids, we're helping to raise them to the same communication level as the rest of us.

Identifying and Selecting Solutions

The same strategies that are useful for identifying unsolved problems can be applied to identifying and choosing solutions to those problems. It turned out that the boy described above, who was able to participate in some linguistic give-and-take, was able to participate to some degree in discussions about potential solutions and was generally able to remember the solutions that were arrived at through Proactive Plan B. So he didn't need solutions recorded in writing for later reference. As with any child, sometimes solutions that at first blush seemed realistic and mutually satisfactory don't actually stand the test of time, necessitating a return to Proactive Plan B to consider alternative solutions. For the girl described above—whose communication skills were more limited— her parents created a problem-solving binder filled with laminated cards depicting in pictures potential solutions for each of the problems depicted on her "problem card." When she signaled that she was hungry, she would turn in her binder to the card containing pictures of her preferred solutions to that problem and point to one. If it became apparent that additional solutions were needed, pictures of additional solutions were added. While the ultimate goal is for the girl to "use her words" to communicate preferred solutions, the rudimentary binder system has helped her communicate with people, explode less, and participate in the process.

And it's the last element—participating in the process—that is perhaps the most important. Often it's said that kids with limited communication skills cannot participate in the process of solving problems, but I find that this typically isn't the case. If adults automatically assume that such kids can't participate, then the kids are relegated to being in the audience as decisions are made about how their problems are to be solved. Many can, in fact, participate, and their participation opens the door to the relationship- and communication-enhancing properties that Plan B brings to their interactions with important people in their lives. Sometimes it just takes a little extra creativity and perhaps some additional resources. To that end, you may (if haven't already) want to check out some of the books by Carol Gray and Kari Dunn listed in the resources section at the end of this book.

By the way, I've used the problem-solving binder with kids whose communication skills were not compromised but who, especially in the heat of the moment, had difficulty recalling how past problems had been solved and how solutions to past problems could be applied to similar problems.

A few other points before we move on. Because some solutions are applicable only to certain specific problems (for example, a hot dog would make good sense for the problem of being hungry, but wouldn't be a great solution for most other problems), sometimes it's a good idea to teach a more general set of solutions to facilitate consideration of more specific ones. Hard to believe, but the vast majority of solutions to problems encountered by human beings fall into one of three general categories: (1) ask for help; (2) meet halfway or give a little; and (3) do it a different way. These categories can simplify things for kids whose communication skills are compromised (many of whom may benefit from having the three possibilities depicted in pictures), as well as for kids whose communication skills are generally intact but who become easily overwhelmed by the universe of potential solutions. These categories can be used to guide and structure the consideration of possible solutions. First you'll want to introduce the categories to your child at an opportune moment; then, when you're trying to generate solutions using Plan B, use the categories as the framework for considering solutions. Let's see what that might look like (by necessity, the example is of a child with relatively intact verbal communication skills):

Parent (Empathy step, using Proactive Plan B): I've noticed that you haven't wanted to go to gymnastics lately. What's up?

Child: I don't like my new coach.

Adult: You don't like your new coach. You mean Ginny? How come?

Child: It's boring. All she has us do is stretch. That's boring.

Adult: Okay, let me make sure I've got this straight. You haven't wanted to go to gymnastics lately because it's boring . . . just a bunch of stretching.

Child: Right.

Adult: Is that the only reason you haven't wanted to go to gymnastics lately?

Child: Uh-huh.

Adult (Define the Problem step): I can understand that. The thing is, you usually really like gymnastics, and you're really good at it, so I'd hate to see you give it up.

Child: I don't care.

Adult: You don't care?

Child: Not if it's just going to be a bunch of stretching.

Adult (Invitation): Well, I wonder if there's a way for us to do something about all that stretching without your giving up gymnastics completely. Do you have any ideas?

Child: Ginny's not going to change the way she does her class.

Adult: You might be right about that. But let's think about our problem-solving options. I don't know if "asking for help" will solve this problem. And I can't think of how we would "meet halfway" or "give a little" on this one, especially if you think

Ginny isn't going to change the way she does her class. I'm thinking this is one where we'd "try to do it a different way." What do you think?

Child: I don't know what a different way would be.

Adult: Well, let's think about it. Ginny's not the only one who teaches that level. The main reason we picked Ginny's class is because the other class that's your level is the same time as your ice skating lesson. But maybe we could change ice skating to a different time. Then you could be in the other gymnastics class. What do you think?

Naturally, this Plan B discussion would continue until a realistic and mutually satisfactory solution has been agreed on. Not only would the problem get solved, Plan B would set the stage, over time, for the child to continue using the problem-solving categories as a framework for generating solutions.

By the way, a talented speech and language therapist can take you much further than I've tried to in this section. Something worth looking into, if you haven't already.

TEACHING SKILLS

Earlier in this book, you learned that lagging skills are the *why* of explosions. But for the last few chapters, we've been primarily focused on unsolved problems (the *who, what, where,* and *when* of explosions). This leads to a very important question: How do you teach the lagging skills if you're primarily working on solving problems?

There are two answers. First, your kid will learn and practice many of the skills he lacks while you're using Plan B to solve problems. Second, Plan B can be the *framework* through which you can teach the remaining lagging skills. Let's think about both.

Skills Taught by Participating in Plan B

Let's start with this Plan B dialogue and then we'll consider whether any lagging skills were being learned and practiced:

Mother: I've heard that you want to go to the football game Friday night with your friends.

Kid: Uh-huh.

Mother: And I heard from your father that you were hoping to go without me or your father as chaperones.

Kid: I can't believe you guys don't trust me enough to go to the football game without you!

Mother: Well, I'm not sure that this is about not trusting you.

Kid: What's it about, then?

Mother: It's really about some of the things that go on at football games that make us a little shaky about having you there without one of us nearby.

Kid: What do you think is going to happen? I don't believe this!

Mother: I guess I'd like to hear about why it's so important to you that we don't accompany you.

Kid: Because you're treating me like I'm a baby! I'm not a baby! I'm a freshman in high school! This is so embarrassing!

Mother: So your main concern is that it's embarrassing for your father or me to accompany you to a football game.

Kid: Yes!

Mother: Nothing else?

Kid: Nothing else. Why don't you guys trust me?

Mother: Like I said, it's not that we don't trust you. It's more that there are things that go on at your high school football games—drinking, fights— that make us uncomfortable about your being there without us.

Kid: I don't do any of those things!

Mother: I know. We just worry about your getting hurt if those things are going on around you.

Kid: My friends don't do those things either.

Mother: Yes, I know. Like I said, it's what's going on around you that we worry about.

Kid: If I can't go without you guys right next to me, then I'm not going.

Mother: Well, I was wondering if there was a way for you to go to the football game without our being right next to you and embarrassing you, but still have your father and me be comfortable about your safety. I'm wondering what that would look like.

Kid: You not worrying so much is what it would look like.

Mother: I know that's your preference. But I'm just wondering if there's a way for us both to get our concerns addressed . . . you know, your not being embarrassed and our feeling like you're safe.

Kid: I don't know! This is so ridiculous!

Mother: Well, let's think about it.

(*Pause*)

Kid: Mr. Abernathy goes to the games. He could keep an eye on us.

Mother: Mr. Abernathy your soccer coach?

Kid: Uh-huh. He said he goes to all the games.

Mother: And you're thinking that if he was willing to keep an eye on you, then we would feel more comfortable about your safety and you wouldn't be embarrassed by your parents hanging around?

Kid: Yep. I mean, I don't want him standing right next to me.

Mother: No, I'd be okay if he was nearby. And you wouldn't be okay if it was me or your father nearby but not next to you?

Kid: That would be so obvious!

Mother: Okay. Let me think about whether this will work for me. We'd need to find out if Mr. Abernathy is willing to keep an eye on you.

Kid: Can you call him?

Mother: I can call him. And your father and I would

drop you off at the game just before it starts and then pick you up right after it's over?

Kid: Yep.

Mother: I don't think it's fair for Mr. Abernathy to keep an eye on you every game. So we'd still need a solution that works for the rest of the games, if you're hoping to go to them. But I don't mind asking him to watch you and your friends for this game. Yes?

Kid: Yes!

Mother: I think this solution will work for your father, too. So let me ask him about that and then I'll call Mr. Abernathy.

Were any lagging skills being worked on and practiced in this example of Plan B? Yes, quite a few, in fact: reflecting on multiple thoughts or ideas simultaneously (the kid's concerns and her mother's concerns were being considered); organization (this was a very structured, organized way to go about solving problems); considering the likely outcomes or consequences of actions (mother and daughter were both thinking about how solutions would pan out and whether they would address the concerns of both parties); considering a range of solutions to a problem (they did consider a few different solutions); expressing concerns, needs, or thoughts in words; managing emotional response to frustration in order to think rationally (it wasn't perfect, but it was better); shifting from an original idea or solution; taking into account situational factors that would suggest the need to adjust a plan of action; changing inflexible, inaccurate interpretations (the daughter did seem to progress beyond the belief that her parents didn't trust her); appreciating how behavior is affecting other people (the solution took both parties' concerns into account); and appreciating another person's perspective or point of view.

When you're using Plan B, you're not just solving a problem; you're working on and practicing lagging skills, too.

Let's think about how Plan B might be helpful for rigid, concrete, black-and-white thinkers in particular, as these kids represent a high percentage of "exploders." As you may recall, such kids have difficulty with grayer aspects of living, such as problem solving, social interactions, and unpredictable circumstances. In different ways, each of the three steps of Plan B can be extremely useful in helping these children handle demands for flexibility and frustration tolerance more adaptively.

The Empathy step is crucial for such children, since they often overreact when faced with the realization that their rigid notions about how events should unfold will not be realized. In many instances, these children put rigid solutions on the table rather than concerns, so clarifying their concerns can create some wiggle room in the solution department. But because their concerns can seem quite unreasonable—even bizarre—to the untrained listener, many of these children have grown accustomed to having adults (and often peers as well) instantaneously dismiss their concerns. Rule number one: no matter how bizarre or illogical their concerns may be to you, they're not bizarre or illogical to the child, so it's extremely important to make sure that the child's concerns are clarified and entered into consideration. This can be very reassuring to a child who's become convinced that his concerns are never taken into account.

The Define the Problem step helps the child do something he's probably never been very good at: taking another person's concerns into account. Once again, the child doesn't have to "own" your concern to assist in solving the problem, and he doesn't even have to care about it; he merely needs to take it into account. Sometimes, helping a rigid, inflexible child simply hear someone else's concern without instantaneously exploding is a major achievement.

Finally, the Invitation step helps the child do something else he's never been very good at: adjusting to the idea that there might be some shades of gray between black and white and that there might be a variety of ways to solve a problem besides the way he originally configured. Early on, this often requires massive doses of reassurance that the child's concern will be taken into account. And such children often benefit from being reminded about how they have solved similar problems in the past.

Plan B as the Framework for an Approach to Teaching Lagging Skills

This section doesn't cover all aspects of teaching lagging skills directly, but it does provide some examples of various skills that probably wouldn't be taught by merely engaging a kid in Plan B, but the teaching of which might be facilitated by using Plan B as the framework for approaching the issue.

Let's take swearing as an example. Swearing is usually a sign that a child doesn't currently have the communication or emotion regulation skills to express himself adaptively in the midst of frustration. You could respond to swearing with "I refuse to be spoken to like that!" or "Go to your room and come back when you're ready to talk to me the right way!" These statements might have an impact if your kid lacked the knowledge that you didn't want to be spoken to that way or wasn't motivated to speak to you the right way. But if your kid lacks communication or emotion regulation skills, then these statements are highly unlikely to accomplish the mission.

There are two ways to reduce swearing. One is to solve the specific problems that precipitate swearing, because once the problems are solved, the kid won't be frustrated about them, so he won't have reason to swear. The other is to directly teach the skill that would replace the swearing. In the latter case, Plan B would create the framework for communicating about the lagging skill and the mechanism for kid and adult to collaborate on a plan of action for working on it. An example:

Mother: We had a bad incident this week, and I'm not sure I handled it well.

Therapist: Tell me.

Mother: Well, I was making pancakes for breakfast. Derrick came into the kitchen and said he didn't want pancakes. I told him that's what was on the menu—

Therapist: Sorry to interrupt, but did you mean to be handling the pancake problem with Plan A?

Mother, smiling: No.

Therapist: Just curious. Go on.

Mother: So then he called me a name and ran out of the kitchen. I ran after him and told him he was grounded for a week for calling me a name. He told me to get away from him. I insisted on an immediate apology. He went ballistic for the next half hour.

Therapist: It sounds extremely unpleasant. You mentioned that you wished you'd handled things differently?

Mother: First off, I shouldn't have been using Plan A on the pancakes—I could have helped him find something else to eat.

Therapist: True, I suppose. Of course, it's hard to respond diplomatically in the heat of the moment. How often does he get upset over what you're making for breakfast?

Mother: All the time! I try to make things I know he likes, but it seems like he doesn't want whatever I'm making most of the time.

Therapist: So this is a pretty predictable problem.

Mother: Absolutely. Almost daily.

Therapist: So one thing we'll want to do is try to solve the breakfast problem proactively rather than emergently. But I take it that's not the only time he swears at you.

Mother: He swears at me whenever he's frustrated.

Therapist: So we have a skill to teach, too. And it's pretty clear that all the punishing isn't teaching that skill. I don't think he needs any more lessons on the importance of not swearing or any more motivation not to swear. At the moment, it seems pretty clear that Derrick isn't very good at expressing his frustration without swearing. So he needs your help.

Mother: So what should I do?

Therapist: I wonder if you and Derrick can use Plan B on the topic of what he can do or say—instead of swearing—when he gets frustrated.

Mother: What would that sound like?

Therapist: It would sound the same as Plan B does when you're working on a problem. But now you're working on a skill. So you might say, "I've noticed that sometimes when you get mad at me you say things that aren't very nice. What's up?" Obviously, this would be better done proactively instead of emergently.

Mother: Sounds doable.

Therapist: Any ideas for what he could do or say

instead, just in case he doesn't come up with anything?

Mother: Well, he could just leave the room without swearing at me. And then we could try to solve whatever problem was upsetting him later.

Therapist: That's interesting. Because he seems halfway there already.

Mother: How do you mean?

Therapist: Well, he did leave the room, and that's progress. Of course, it was after he'd already sworn at you that he left the room. So we need to work on getting him to leave the room before he swears at you. And on helping him come up with and practice other words to let you know he's mad.

Difficulty with sharing is another common cause of explosions. Sharing requires a variety of different skills, such as attending to social nuances (for example, noticing that a playmate is feeling left out or bored) and appreciating the impact of one's behavior on others. Here's how Proactive Plan B might sound in addressing these lagging skills:

Parent: Jen, I noticed that your friend Susie was watching you play your computer game during your play-date this afternoon. Was she having a good time?

Jen: I don't know. I guess so.

Parent: How could you tell if she was having a good time?

Jen: I don't know. It's not like she was mad or anything.

Parent: No, she didn't look mad. I thought maybe she might have been a little bored.

Jen: She likes playing computer games.

Parent: Well, that's just the thing. She wasn't really playing the computer game—she was watching you play.

Jen: She likes watching me play.

Parent: I wasn't too sure about that. But I wonder if there's a way for us to find out if Susie is happy watching you play the next time she comes over.

Jen: I could ask her.

Parent: Yes, you could ask her. And if she says she'd like to play—instead of just watching—will you let her?

Jen: Yes, as long as she didn't play too long.

Parent: Ah, so you wouldn't want to watch her for very long. I wonder if that's how Susie was feeling when she was watching you.

Jen: Maybe.

Parent: So would you like my help, the next time Susie comes over, figuring out how long one of you should play and the other should watch so no one has to watch for too long? Or would like to do that on your own?

Jen: I think I need your help.

Parent: Okay. I can do that. Would you also like me to say something to you—you know, quietly—if I'm worried that Susie might not be having such a good time? Just in case you don't notice. What do you think?

Jen: Okay.

One final example: some kids interpret social information in a distorted, biased, rigid, inaccurate manner (for example, "It's not fair!" "You always blame me!" "Nobody likes me," or "I'm stupid"). These interpretations can cause spontaneous combustion if left unattended.

Entire books have been written on how to restructure the inaccurate, maladaptive thoughts of children and adults. The idea is to help the individual recognize the inaccuracy of his existing belief systems and replace the inaccurate thoughts that make up these belief systems with a more accurate, adaptive way of thinking. This restructuring usually involves "disconfirming" the individual's old thoughts by systematically presenting evidence that is contrary to these rigid beliefs. Let's think about what it might sound like if Plan B were used to provide a framework for addressing this issue.

Adult: Cindy, I've noticed you haven't been too enthusiastic about going to school lately. What's up?

Cindy: I hate school.

Adult: Yes, I've heard you say that before. What is it about school that you hate?

Cindy: I just don't like it.

Adult: That's a shame, because you have to spend a lot of time there. But what is it that you don't like?

Cindy: The other kids think I'm stupid.

Adult: They do? How so?

Cindy: They just do.

Adult: Tell me what you mean by "stupid."

Cindy: You know, dumb, stupid.

Adult: What makes you think the other kids think you're stupid? Do they say you're stupid?

Cindy: No, not exactly. I just know they think that.

Adult: Well, there must be some reason you think the other kids think you're stupid. What made you decide that?

Cindy: I'm not very good in reading.

Adult: Ah, yes, I know that's something you're working on. But I guess you still don't feel like you're so good at it.

Cindy: Well, I'm still in the lowest reading group.

Adult: And that's making you feel like you're stupid?

Cindy: Uh-huh.

Adult: Are you stupid in math?

Cindy: No. I'm good in math.

Adult: Interesting. You're good in math but you're still "stupid" because you feel that you're not so good in reading.

Cindy: Right.

Adult: See, here's the thing. I'm not sure how you could be good in math and still be stupid.

Cindy: Well, I am.

Adult: I wonder if there's a way for you to be good in math and not as good in reading without feeling stupid.

Cindy: Huh?

Adult: I wonder what you could say—instead of "I'm stupid"—to let people know that you're good in math but still working on reading.

Cindy: I don't know.

Adult: Well, let's think about it. There's no rush.

Cindy: Um . . . how 'bout, "I'm good in math but I'm still working on the reading part."

Adult: Sounds good to me. Should I remind you of that next time you say you're stupid?

Cindy: Um . . . okay.

Inaccurate interpretations can't be "fixed" in one shot. But you can work on and improve them over time. Plan B provides a framework for getting started.

Q & A

Question: If I choose to medicate my child, how long will he be on the medication?

Answer: That's hard to predict. The chemical effects of psychotropic medication endure only as long as the medication is taken. However, in some children, the behavioral improvements that are facilitated by medication persist even after the medications are discontinued, especially if a child has acquired new, compensatory skills. Ultimately, the question of whether a child should remain on medication must be continuously revisited.

Question: How do you feel about homeopathic and natural remedies?

Answer: I've seen parents who feel better about using such remedies instead of prescribed medication, and I've seen some kids benefit from them, so there's no reason to dismiss these agents. I don't like to see people stick with any intervention if it's not helpful, if they're receiving care from someone who isn't competent, if the intervention is doing more harm than good, or if there are interventions that might be more effective. Of course, I apply the same mentality to prescribed medication, too.

Question: For how long should I use Plan B? How much progress should I expect from my child, and how fast?

Answer: Well, let's think about what you're doing. You're solving problems collaboratively so you and your child won't fight about those problems anymore. You're communicating with your child. You're improving your relationship. You're letting him know that you're not the only one with good ideas about how to solve problems, that he has good ideas, too. You're teaching him that his concerns are valid, and that yours are, too. And you're letting him know that you're as invested in ensuring that his concerns are addressed as you are in getting your own concerns addressed. Now why would you want to stop doing all that, even if he's not exploding anymore?

A lot of parents begin to use the approach described in this book thinking that eventually they'll be able to get back to Plan A again. In reality, as parents and children get better at Plan B and as their relationship improves, the importance of Plan A actually diminishes. Over time most parents don't miss Plan A, and they definitely don't long for the "good old days."

Children and parents vary widely in terms of how quickly they respond to this approach. The first goal is to take the fuel out of the fire as quickly as possible by dramatically decreasing the use of Plan A and dramatically increasing the use of Plan B and Plan C. This shift in the way you respond to and communicate with your child should correspond with a decrease in the frequency, duration, and intensity of explosions. And, of course, an increase in the use of Proactive Plan B also means that numerous problems are getting solved. Some families are able to achieve this in a few weeks, some take several months, and others take longer still. Some children continue to have occasional, residual explosions for a few months, but such episodes are often far less intense and fizzle out a lot faster. The goal is for things to be better.

Question: Should I reward my child for participating in Plan B?

Answer: Fewer explosions and getting along better with you are usually reward enough.

Question: Does using this approach mean that rewards and punishments are completely out of the picture?

Answer: Not necessarily. But by now you should have a very realistic sense of what rewards and punishments can and can't help you achieve and an awareness of the special care required when imposing consequences on an explosive child. The real question is this: Will additional motivation enhance your child's performance at any point along the way? The answer: probably not. But let's think about it.

The first thing you'd want to be sure about is whether your child actually needs additional motivation. The philosophy of the CPS approach—children do well if they can—suggests that your child is already sufficiently motivated. Second, you'd want to be sure that motivational strategies are worth the potential price. Many an explosion has been precipitated by the delivery of a punishment or the loss of an anticipated reward. Engaging children in discussions about how they can make amends for an act committed in the midst of frustration can be far more productive than punishment. Such discussions should not take place during or immediately after explosions but rather once rational thinking has been fully restored.

Question: What about time-out?

Answer: Some children actually find time-out to be a good place to calm down when they're frustrated, although I find this to be the exception, since time-out is usually used as a punishment. More commonly, the explosions of many children are actually exacerbated—sometimes dramatically so—if someone makes any kind of physical contact with them while they're frustrated. So if time-out simply fuels your child's explosions, forget it. Even under optimal circumstances, time-out is generally not recommended for older children and adolescents.

On the other hand, it can be productive to help parents and children agree to go their separate ways—with each going to different designated rooms of the house—when it becomes obvious that a discussion is going poorly or is not going to be resolved immediately. Not all explosive children will follow through on this plan, but a surprising number will. The discussion resumes after everyone has calmed down and had a chance to think a little.

Question: But I still have the feeling that some of my child's behavior is planned and willful. How do I tell the difference?

Answer: I'm not sure it's going to be possible to determine with great precision whether your kid's behavior is planned or unplanned, and you certainly don't want to try to figure this out in the heat of the moment. There are essentially two possible mistakes you can make. The first is to think your child's behavior is unplanned and unintentional when it really isn't. The second is thinking your child's behavior is planned and intentional when it really isn't. If you have to make an error, make the first error. In other words, when in doubt, respond as if your child's behavior is unplanned and unintentional. The ramifications of the second error—and how it influences your response—are much more serious.

Question: My child becomes frustrated about things that don't involve interactions with me or other people. He just gets really frustrated with something he's doing, like playing with his Wii. Or sometimes he has a delayed response to a frustration that happened earlier in the day. What then?

Answer: It's true, there may be times when your child's frustration doesn't involve you or another person. And there are instances in which a child's frustration at the moment is a delayed response to an earlier frustration, such as something that happened in school. But your role remains the same: to identify the unsolved problem and try to solve it with Plan B.

Mother, standing on the front walk to the house: Charlotte, we're waiting for you to get in the car so we can go to the beach.

Charlotte, standing in the front doorway: I'm not going.

Mother: What? Charlotte, you love the beach.

Charlotte, backing into the house: I said I'm not going!

Mother, moving toward the front door, and using Plan A: Charlotte, your brother and father are already in the car, we're in a hurry, and I don't feel like going through this with you right now! Go get me my keys and let's go!

Charlotte, slamming and locking the front door to the house: Stay away from me! I'm not going!

Mother, still using Plan A: Charlotte, you unlock this door right now! (*Turning to husband in car*) Honey, do you have your keys?

Husband: No. Why?

Mother, pulse pounding, turning back to the locked front door, still using Plan A: Charlotte, open the door, damn it! This isn't funny! (No response from inside the house.)

Father, arriving at front door: What's going on?

Mother, through gritted teeth: Your daughter has informed me that she's not going to the beach and has locked us out of our house.

Hmm. That actually looks like an example of how not to do it. Now, let's rewind the tape and try a different approach.

Mother, standing on the front walk to the house: Charlotte, we're waiting for you to get in the car so we can go to the beach.

Charlotte: I'm not going.

Mother, using the Empathy step: You're not going?

Charlotte: No, I'm not going!

Mother: What's the matter, honey?

Charlotte, rubbing her eyes: I just don't want to go.

Mother, squatting down to Charlotte's level: Is there something about going to the beach today that's bothering you? You usually can't wait to go to the beach.

Charlotte: It's too early to go to the beach!

Mother: I don't know what you mean that it's too early to go to the beach.

Charlotte: We don't usually go to the beach until after church. We never go to the beach in the morning.

Mother: It's bothering you that we don't usually go to the beach in the morning.

Charlotte: We never go to the beach in the morning. We can't go right now.

Mother, defining the problem: I'm glad you told me what's the matter. The thing is, we're all ready to go. But let's think about this a little. Maybe we can figure out what to do.

Question: My child has to have each solution spelled out in perfect detail. Is this normal?

Answer: Many explosive kids don't handle ambiguity in their lives well, and this extends to their solutions to problems. Statements like "Okay, we'll do that later" or "We'll go there soon" or "You can do that for a while" have the potential to fuel their frustration, even in the context of Plan B. Here's an example of how such vague statements can backfire:

Trent, sitting in the backseat of the family car: I need something to eat.

Mother, in the role of genius and lucking out, temporarily: We'll stop for something very soon.

Trent: Okay.

[Five minutes of silence elapse.]

Trent, with agitation: I thought you said we were stopping to eat!

Mother: I said we'd stop soon.

Trent, with significantly greater agitation: I can't wait! You said we were stopping!

Father, choosing Plan A over Emergency Plan B: Your mother said we'd stop soon; now put a lid on it!

Trent, very loudly, kicking the back of his father's seat: You guys are such freaking liars! You always do this! You say you'll do something, and then you don't!

Mother, still not using Empathy: Look, we'll stop for food as soon as we can.

[Kaboom.]

On a related topic, some kids don't adapt well when a solution doesn't solve a problem as well as expected. Mike, a remarkably rigid thirteen-year-old, had agreed with his mother over when (twelve noon on Saturday) and how (with her help) he'd clean his room. Mike was actually eager to get his room straightened up, but he lacked the organizational skills to do it on his own. Unfortunately, his mother was delayed by another commitment and wasn't around at twelve noon to help Mike clean his room. This change in plan proved to be a major obstacle for Mike. When the mother arrived home at 1:30 p.m. and suggested that they begin cleaning the room, Mike was very agitated. At 1:31 his mother insisted that they clean the room. Mike's agitation increased. His mother insisted further. At 1:32 things exploded. What Mike needed was a complete reconfiguring of the original solution. He was just that rigid.

Question: Many of the examples I've read so far relate to younger children. My explosive child is fifteen. Any special suggestions?

Answer: Actually, I've been intentionally nonspecific about kids' ages in most of the examples throughout this book. Believe it or not, your child's chronological age is not the key issue. His developmental age in the domains of flexibility, frustration tolerance, and problem solving is the key issue. While the language we'd use would probably be more sophisticated for many fifteen-year-olds than for four-year-olds, the emphasis on solving problems and teaching skills would be exactly the same. Kids respond to being understood and to a collaborative approach regardless of age.

Question: How come my child explodes at home but not at school? Doesn't that prove he can hold it together when he feels like it?

Answer: More than likely it proves something we already knew: that he explodes only under certain conditions. But schools also have a few advantages over homes. The schedule is more predictable (that's helpful for some explosive kids), there's less unstructured time (that's helpful for some explosive kids), and your child's medicine (especially if it's a stimulant) is in full effect during school hours. But the main advantage schools have is the embarrassment factor: your child is keeping himself very tightly wrapped at school because he doesn't want to embarrass himself. Then he gets home and unravels because he's put so much energy into staying tightly wrapped at school. He can't keep himself tightly wrapped twenty-four hours a day. Homes aren't as structured and predictable as most schools, and homes don't have the embarrassment factor.

Question: My child is exploding at school, and I don't think the teachers have heard of this model. Advice?

Answer: Sounds like your child is blowing through the embarrassment factor. Schools (not all but most) tend to be bastions of Plan A. You'll have to make sure they get exposed to this model. More on this in chapter 11.

Question: There are many problems that haven't been mentioned yet—lying, stealing, drug use, unsafe sex. How would those problems be handled using Plan B?

Answer: The steps are the same, and the Empathy step may be the hardest. Don't forget that many difficult issues will require more than one Plan B conversation. Sometimes you won't arrive at the solution that ends up solving the problem durably until after you've tried a few other solutions to the problem. But here's what a Proactive Plan B conversation might look like on the lying issue:

Adult: I've noticed that sometimes it's hard for you to tell me the truth about some things.

Child: Like what?

Adult: Well, the other day I asked you if your homework was done, and you told me it was. So I let you keep playing your video game. But I got a note from Mrs. Nixon today that your homework actually wasn't done.

Child: She's lying!

Adult: She could be lying, I guess. But I've noticed that you were having trouble telling the truth about some other things that had nothing to do with Mrs. Nixon.

Child: What else?

Adult: Um, when I called home from my meeting last week, I asked you if you had mowed the lawn, and you told me you had. And then I got home and the lawn wasn't mowed. Remember?

Child: Well, I meant to mow the lawn before you got home, but I didn't get to it.

Adult: I understand how that could happen. The thing is, when you lie to me about those things, it makes me feel like I can't trust you on other things.

Child: Okay, I won't lie anymore!

Adult: That would be wonderful. But I think I'd feel a little more confident about that if I understood why you were having trouble telling me the truth in the first place.

Child: I don't want you to get mad at me and punish me.

Adult: Ah, you don't want me to get mad and punish you. I can understand that. I guess I can get pretty mad about things, can't I?

Child: Yup.

Adult: I wonder if there's a way for you to not worry about me getting mad and punishing you so that I can trust you to tell me the truth. Do you have any ideas?

Child: You could promise not to get mad and punish me.

Adult: I could promise that. I'm trying very hard not to punish you anymore because it doesn't seem to be helping. Have you noticed?

Child: Sorta.

Adult: But I don't know if I can promise that I'll never get mad at you again. I might slip sometimes. I can promise to try very hard not to get mad at you.

Child: I could promise to try very hard not to lie to you.

Adult: So we both have something to work on, don't we?

Child: Yup.

Adult: What should we do if I slip up and get mad?

Child: I could remind you of your promise.

Adult: That would be very helpful. What should I do if you slip up and tell me a lie?

Child: You could remind me of my promise.

Adult: I think we've got a plan. Let's see how it works. If it doesn't work too well, we'll talk again and see if we can figure out what to do instead.

Child: Okay.

What if you thought that your adolescent daughter was having sex with her boyfriend and you had some concerns about that? With Plan A you're starting the conversation by saying "You must not have sex with your boyfriend," in which case the conversation wouldn't take place because you ended it already. With Plan C you're not having the conversation because you're not raising the topic. And here's what it looks like with Plan B:

Parent: Can we talk about something?

Daughter: Like what?

Parent: Like you and Kenny.

Daughter: Oh, no, here we go again.

Parent: No, wait, I just want to talk. I'm not going to lecture you.

Daughter: Yeah, right.

Parent: No, I'm serious. This is not the beginning of a sermon. I just want to understand.

Daughter: I do not want to talk about this with you.

Parent: I know. This isn't exactly a walk in the park for me, either. But I'm concerned about you.

Daughter: What are you concerned about? I'm fine.

Parent: I'm concerned . . . Okay, I'll just say it . . . I'm concerned about whether you're ready for everything that goes along with being in a relationship.

Daughter: Like what?

Parent: Like, you know, the physical part.

Daughter: I'm not talking about this with you! This is none of your business!

Parent: Can you just bear with me for one second? Even if it's none of my business.

Daughter: No! I don't want to talk about this with you!

Parent: Maybe we should find a better time to talk about it.

Daughter: There is no good time to talk about this!

Parent: But can I just tell you what I'm concerned about?

Daughter: Fine, tell me what you're concerned about.

Parent: I know there's a lot of pressure on kids these days to do stuff, and I was just concerned that maybe you were feeling pressured.

Daughter: How do you know what I'm doing with Kenny?

Parent: I don't.

Daughter: So how do you know I feel pressured?

Parent: I don't. That's what I was asking about.

Daughter: It's not that big a deal.

Parent: Okay. But the question is whether you feel pressured, whether you're comfortable with everything you and Kenny are doing.

Daughter: I don't know. I don't want to lose him. And I think this conversation is almost over.

Parent: We can end this conversation whenever you want. But I do get the feeling that you are feeling some pressure and that you may not be completely comfortable with everything you're doing.

Daughter: Maybe. But what can you do about it?

Parent: Maybe nothing. But I'm your mom. And if you don't want to talk to me about these things, I'm okay with that. But I don't want you to feel alone. Not if you're doing things you're not comfortable with because you're afraid of losing Kenny.

Daughter: So who should I talk to? Some shrink?

Parent: I don't know. Can we talk about that a little?

Daughter: I think this is enough for right now.

Parent: Can we talk again?
Daughter: I'll think about it.

Believe it or not, this is a good beginning. Plan B is not the mechanical exercise of getting through three steps. It's a process of gathering information, sharing concerns, and thinking about solutions. But Plan B hasn't failed just because you didn't make it through all three steps in the first try.

Question: I'm too tired to do this. I'm sick of my child and I don't have the energy to do all the talking and problem solving you've described. Any advice?

Answer: We need to figure out how to get you your energy back. I've seen the approach described in this book accomplish just that. As parents begin to understand their child's difficulties and respond in a more productive fashion, then the child begins to explode less. Then the parent starts to feel a greater sense of empowerment. As things continue to go well, the parent begins to feel more energized and optimistic.

But it's also the case that some parents need to focus on themselves (sometimes with a therapist), find ways to spend time away from the child and recharge, and find ways to focus on other aspects of life besides the child. Mental health clinicians, support groups, social service agencies, spouses, relatives, and friends can sometimes be of help.

10

Family Matters

Every family has its challenges. Siblings don't always get along, parents don't always see eye to eye on things, everyone's too busy, kids are stressed about school or grades or friends, adults are stressed about work or money or marriage or life in general, and just about everyone's stressed about homework.

Add an explosive child to the mix, and you'll push many families and marriages to the brink. Small annoyances turn into big problems, minor disagreements and stressors become major catastrophes, and communication problems that might never have been noticed become glaring roadblocks. Next, add grandparents who remember the way they would've done things in the good old days and soccer or hockey coaches or teachers who are delighted to tell you how they'd handle your kid, and life has suddenly become much more interesting than what most people signed up for. So now it's not just the explosive kid you're dealing with, it's a whole bunch of folks.

And while all of that may feel very overwhelming at times, it might help you to know that we're going to deal with all those folks the same way we've been trying to deal with the problems that need to be solved with your explosive child: one at a time.

SIBLINGS

Run-of-the-mill sibling rivalry can look like a walk in the park when one of the siblings is explosive. And while it's not uncommon for "ordinary" siblings to direct their greatest hostility and most savage acts toward each other, these acts can be more intense, frequent, and traumatizing when one of the siblings is explosive. In addition, though it's not unusual for "ordinary" siblings to complain about preferential treatment and disparities in parental attention and expectations, these issues can be magnified in families with an explosive child because he may consume such a disproportionate share of the parents' resources.

So we have a few very important agenda items here. We want to protect siblings from the verbal and physical aggression of their explosive brother or sister. But we also want to recognize that while the explosive child's response to difficult sibling interactions is way over the top, those interactions involve two people. In other words, it typically takes two to tango. We want to make sure that siblings get the attention and time and nurturing they need from you. But we also understand that the explosive kid may require a disproportionate share of that attention and time and nurturing, at least until we get some problems solved and some skills taught. We want to make sure that siblings understand why their brother or sister is having so much trouble being flexible, tolerating frustration, and solving problems. But we don't want them to feel like they're walking on eggshells or that their needs and concerns always take a backseat to the seemingly more pressing needs of the explosive child. And we want to make sure that the siblings know that we appreciate how hard it is to have an explosive brother or sister. But we need to empathize in a way that isn't disrespectful or dismisses the very significant and real needs of the explosive child.

You have your work cut out for you.

Fortunately, Plan B can improve interactions among siblings. If they are old enough to comprehend, it is often useful to help brothers and sisters understand why their explosive sibling acts the way he does, why his behavior is so difficult to change, how to interact with him in a way that reduces hostility and minimizes the likelihood of aggression or explosions, and what the parents are actively doing to try to improve things. Brothers and sisters tend to be more receptive if there's an improvement in the general tone of family interactions and if the explosive sibling is blowing up less often and becomes an active participant in making things better.

However, this understanding doesn't always keep siblings from complaining about an apparent double standard between themselves and their explosive brother or sister. Armed with the knowledge that parental attention is never distributed with 100 percent parity and that parental priorities are never exactly the same for each child in any family, you should resist responding to this complaint by trying even harder to treat your explosive child the same as you do your other children. In all families—yours and everyone else's—*fair does not mean equal*. Even parents in "ordinary" families often find themselves helping one child more with homework, having higher academic expectations for one child, or being more nurturing toward another. In your family, you're doing things a little differently for the child who needs extra help in the areas of flexibility, frustration tolerance, and problem solving, but you're also doing things differently for the other children, who have challenges and needs of their own. So when siblings complain about disparities in parental expectations, it's an excellent opportunity to empathize and educate.

Sister: How come you don't get mad at Danny when he swears at you? It's not fair!

Mother: I know that it's very hard for you to listen to him swearing. I don't like it very much, either. But in our family we try to help one another and make sure everyone gets what he or she needs. I'm trying to help Danny solve some frustrating problems and to help him think of different words he could use instead of swearing. That's what he needs help with.

Sister: But swearing is bad. You should get mad at him when he swears.

Mother: Well, I don't get mad at you when I'm helping you with your math, right? That's because I don't think getting mad at you would help very much. Remember how I used to get mad at Danny whenever he swore? It didn't work very well, did it? It just made things worse. So I'm doing something now that I think will eventually work better. I think it's starting to work pretty well.

Sister: What are you going to do if I start swearing?

Mother: I'd help you think of different words, too. Then again, you don't seem to have a problem with swearing, which is really good. So it doesn't look like that's what you need my help with.

Sister: Yes. Math is what I need help with.

Mother: Exactly.

What should you do to resolve disputes between siblings? Apply Plan B. The ingredients are the same, except that the adults' role is that of Plan B facilitator. You'll still want to take it one problem at a time. And because problems between siblings tend to be highly predictable, Proactive Plan B is still far preferable to Emergency Plan B. You'll want to ensure that the concerns of both siblings are entered into consideration. (Often this is better accomplished by doing the Empathy step in separate discussions with both siblings prior to bringing them together to discuss potential solutions.) And you'll still want to make sure that the agreed-on solutions truly address the concerns of both parties and are realistic and mutually satisfactory.

Over time, siblings of explosive kids feel better when problems are resolved through Plan B because they're seeing that their concerns are truly being heard, understood, and taken into account. Over time, they come to see their explosive sibling as more approachable and less terrifying. And they appreciate being involved in the process of working toward solutions and come to recognize that you're able to handle the process in an even-handed manner.

Here's what Plan B between two siblings—with a parent as facilitator—looks like:

Preliminary Plan B with Sibling #1 (Sibling #2 is not present):

Parent: I've noticed that you and your brother are fighting a lot when you're in the playroom together. What's up?

Andrew: Caleb always plays with my toys.

Parent: Ah, so you don't want him playing with your toys. But I thought we were keeping your toys in your bedroom and his toys in his bedroom . . . so I thought the toys in the playroom were for sharing.

Andrew: Right.

Parent: So I don't think I understand what you mean when you say "your" toys.

Andrew: The ones I'm playing with.

Parent: Ah, so Caleb tries to play with the toys that you're still playing with.

Andrew: Uh-huh.

Parent: Does he know you're still playing with them?

Andrew: I don't know. He doesn't ask me.

Parent: How would he be able to tell you're still playing with them?

Andrew: I don't know.

Parent: Can you give me an example of a toy that you might be playing with and then he starts playing with it?

Andrew: The cars.

Parent: Ah, the cars. So you'll be playing with the cars and then he'll butt in and want to play with them, too?

Andrew: Well, I'm not exactly playing with them. But I'm not done with them yet.

Parent: Oh, I see. So you're not still using them but you're also not done with them. Yes?

Andrew: Yes.

Parent: How would Caleb know you're not done with them if you're not still using them?

Andrew: I don't know.

Parent: And how much time should pass when you're not playing with them before you're through with them?

Andrew: I don't know.

Parent: Okay, I think I understand. I'm going to talk to Caleb about this, too, because fighting over the toys is making you guys hurt each other and that's not okay in our house.

Andrew: Okay.

Preliminary Plan B with Sibling #2 (Sibling #1 is not present):

Parent: Caleb, can we talk a little about what's going on between you and Andrew when you guys are playing together?

Caleb: Okay.

Parent: Why do you think you guys are fighting so much sometimes?

Caleb: He won't let me play with the toys I want to play with.

Parent: How come he won't let you play with the toys you want to play with?

Caleb: He says he's still playing with them. But he's not still playing with them! And then there's nothing for me to play with!

Parent: So it seems like he's still playing with everything?

Caleb: Yes!

Parent: So you're not trying to play with what he's playing with right then?

Caleb: No, I'm trying to play with something else! But

he says he's still playing with everything I try to play with!

Parent: So there's nothing left to play with.

Caleb: Uh-huh. Then he hits me when I try to play with something.

Parent: We need to solve this problem, don't we?

Caleb: Yes, because I never get to play with anything if Andrew's around.

Parent: I think we need to have a meeting with Andrew so we can talk about it.

Plan B continues with Siblings #1 and #2 together:

Parent: I've talked with both of you about the playing together problem, and I thought it would be good to come up with a solution together. Andrew, you told me that sometimes you're still playing with toys even though you're not exactly using them, yes?

Andrew: Yes.

Parent: And Caleb, you told me that there's so many toys that Andrew is still playing with that there's nothing left for you to play with, yes?

Caleb: Uh-huh.

Parent: And I'm concerned because when you guys are having trouble sharing toys, you end up hitting each other and someone gets hurt, and that's not the way I want people to treat each other in our family.

Caleb: He hits me first!

Andrew: I wouldn't hit you if you didn't touch stuff I'm still playing with!

Parent: Um . . . I don't know if we'll ever figure out who hits who first. I do think we can solve this problem, though, so no one's hitting anyone. I wonder if there's a way for Caleb to know what toys you're still playing with, Andrew, but still have some toys to play with himself. Do you guys have any ideas?

Andrew: He could stay out of the room I'm playing in.

Parent: Well, that's one idea. But if you're in the playroom, and Caleb isn't allowed in there while you're in there, I don't know if that would be fair to Caleb.

Andrew: But he has toys in his room! He could play with them. And then he wouldn't touch mine.

Caleb: I don't want to play with the toys in my room all the time! I want to play with the toys in the playroom sometimes!

Parent: So, Andrew, let's hold on to that solution just in case we can't come up with anything else. Any other ideas for how we could know what toys Andrew is still playing with but still have some toys for Caleb to play with?

Andrew: I could tell him what toys I'm still playing with.

Caleb: You already do that . . . and it's everything!

Andrew: Well, I'm not through playing with everything yet!

Parent: Andrew, how long does it take for you to be done playing with something?

Andrew: I don't know.

Parent: Like, we're sitting here talking right now. And you haven't been in the playroom since this morning. Is there anything you're still playing with in the playroom?

Andrew: Um . . . the cars.

Caleb: No way! He hasn't been in there since this morning!

Andrew: Yeah, but I have them set up a certain way and I don't want you to wreck 'em!

Parent: So I wonder what we could do about this. Andrew, it's really not fair to Caleb if you're never through playing with the cars. And Caleb, I suppose it's not so terrible for you to not play with the cars if Andrew has them set up a certain way and doesn't want you to wreck the set-up. This is a hard one!

Caleb: At school, you're done playing with a toy when playtime ends.

Parent: Hmm. So when playtime ends, it's a fresh start on who's playing with the toys?

Caleb: Uh-huh. That's how it is at school. But not here.

Parent: Well, maybe it could work here. Andrew, maybe we need a time-limit on how long you're still playing with toys that you haven't used in a while. What do you think?

Andrew: How long?

Parent: I don't know, that's for you guys to decide. I'm wondering what you think of the idea.

Andrew: Maybe it could work.

Caleb: I think he should be done playing with a toy as soon as he's not using it anymore.

Parent: That might be a little quick for Andrew. What do you think, Andrew?

Andrew: Ten minutes. If I haven't used a toy for ten minutes, I'm through playing with it.

Parent: Caleb, what do you think?

Caleb: That would give me a lot more toys to play with.

Parent: Andrew, this could be very hard for you. Caleb would be able to play with the cars you have set up right now because it's been a lot longer than ten minutes since you used them. Can you do that?

Andrew: Maybe Caleb would listen to me if I asked him not to play with the cars because I have them set up . . . but he could play with everything else.

Parent: Caleb, could you do that?

Caleb: Yes, if he told me. But he doesn't tell me. He just tells me I can't play with anything!

Parent: So let's think about what we're deciding here. Andrew, if you haven't used something for ten minutes, then you're through playing with it.

> And Caleb, if Andrew tells you that he's set
> something up in an extra-special way, then you'll
> try not to play with it. Yes?
>
> **Andrew:** Yes.
>
> **Caleb:** Uh-huh.
>
> **Parent:** Well, we'll have to see how this solution
> works. If it doesn't, don't start hitting each other;
> just let me know so we can keep working on it.

Be forewarned that in some instances the behavior of seemingly angelic siblings can begin to deteriorate just as the behavior of their explosive brother or sister begins to improve. This is often a sign that the emotional needs of the siblings—which had been below the radar while the family dealt with the pressing issues of the explosive child—require closer examination. In some cases, therapy may be necessary for brothers and sisters who have been traumatized by their explosive sibling or who may be manifesting other problems that can be traced back to the old family atmosphere.

If you feel that your family needs more help working on these issues than this small section provides, a skilled family therapist can be of great assistance. You may also wish to read an excellent book, *Siblings Without Rivalry*, by Adele Faber and Elaine Mazlish.

COMMUNICATION PATTERNS

A family therapist can also help when it comes to making some fundamental changes in how you communicate with your child. Dealing effectively with an explosive child is easier (not easy, *easier*) when there are healthy patterns of communication between the kid and his parents. When these patterns are unhealthy, dealing effectively with such a child is much harder. As you might imagine, some of these patterns are more typical of older explosive kids. But the seeds may be sown early. Although not an exhaustive list, here's a sampling of some of the more common patterns.

Parents and children sometimes get into a vicious cycle—called *speculation*—of drawing erroneous conclusions about each other's motives or thoughts. Others have referred to this pattern as *psychologizing* or *mind reading*, and it can sound something like this:

> *Parent: The reason Oscar doesn't listen to us is that he thinks he's so much smarter than we are.*

Now, it's not uncommon for people to make inaccurate inferences about one another. Indeed, responding effectively to these inaccuracies—in other words, setting people straight about yourself in a manner they can understand—is a real talent and requires some big-time emotion regulation and communication skills. While there are some kids who are able to respond to speculation by making appropriate, corrective statements to set the record straight ("Dad, I don't think that's true at all"), an explosive kid may hear himself being talked about inaccurately and become extremely frustrated. This is an undesirable circumstance in and of itself, but it's especially undesirable because whether Oscar thinks he's smarter than his parents isn't really the point. In fact, this topic is a red herring that just distracts everyone from working collaboratively toward solutions to the unsolved problems that are setting the stage for Oscar's challenging behavior. Of course, speculation can be a two-way street. From a child's mouth, it might sound something like this:

Oscar: The only reason you guys get so mad at me so much is because you like pushing me around.

Such statements can have the same detour effect, especially when adults follow the careening kid straight through the flashing lights and barriers and right off the cliff:

Mother: Yes, that's exactly right: our main goal in life is to push you around. I can't believe you'd say that, after all we've been through with you.

Oscar: Well, what is your main goal then?

Father: Our main goal is to help you be normal.

Oscar: So now I'm not normal. Thank you very much, loser.

Father: Don't you get disrespectful with me, pal.

Speculation is a no-win proposition. Collaborative Problem Solving is a win-win proposition. So let's stick to the CPS script, and instead of *speculating* on what another family member is thinking or feeling, we'll *drill* for that information instead. That takes a lot of the guesswork (and speculating) out of the mix. In the Empathy step, you're trying to get your kid's concerns on the table. In the Define the Problem step, it's your turn. No psychologizing. No mind-reading. No value judgments. Just pure, unadulterated concerns.

Another maladaptive communication pattern—called *overgeneralization*—refers to the tendency to draw global conclusions in response to isolated events. Here's how it would sound from a parent:

> **Mother:** Kevin, can you please explain to me why you never do your homework?
>
> **Kevin:** What are you talking about?! I do my homework every night!
>
> **Mother:** Your teachers told me you have a few missing assignments this semester.
>
> **Kevin:** So does everybody! What's the big deal? I miss a few assignments, and you're ready to call in the damn cavalry!
>
> **Mother:** Why do you always give me such a hard time? I just want what's best for you.
>
> **Kevin:** Stay out of my damn business! That's what's best for me!

What a shame, because there may actually be ways in which Kevin's mother could help him with his homework or at least get some of the reassurance she was looking for about his completion of homework assignments—not by starting the discussion with an overgeneralization, though. While other children are sometimes able to bypass their parents' overgeneralizations and get to the real issues, many explosive children react strongly to such statements and may lack the skills to respond appropriately with corrective information. Phrasing things in the most neutral way possible should help you overgeneralize less often ("Oliver, I wonder if we can talk about this without screaming at each other" or "Chad, you'll let me know if there's anything about your homework I can help you with?" or "Elizabeth, I don't want to bug you about your homework; can we figure out some way for me to know if it's actually getting done?").

Another common tendency, *perfectionism*, sometimes prevents parents from acknowledging the progress their child has made and makes them cling to an old, unmodified vision of the child's capabilities. Perfectionism is often driven less by the child's lack of progress and more by the parents' own anxiety. Wherever it's coming from, perfectionism is usually counterproductive when applied to a child who may be tired of receiving feedback on practically everything he does or who may feel enormously frustrated by his parents' unrealistic expectations:

Father: Eric, your mother and I are pretty pleased about how much better you're doing in school,

but you're still not working as hard as you ought
to be.

Eric: Huh?

Mother: But that's not what we wanted to talk to you
about. You're staying up too late doing your
homework.

Eric: I get it done, don't I?

Father: Yes, apparently you do, but we want you to
get it done earlier so you get more sleep.

Eric: I get enough sleep.

Father: We don't think you do. You're very grouchy
in the morning, and you have trouble waking up.
We want you to do your homework when you get
home from school from now on.

Eric: I'm not doing my homework when I get home
from school! I need a break when I get home
from school! What difference does it make?

Mother: It makes a difference to us. Now, your father
and I have already talked this over, so there's no
discussion on it. You need to get your homework
done when you get home from school.

Eric: No freaking way.

Hmm. Eric may or may not actually be interested in
thinking about how to get his homework done earlier.
Either way, perfectionism (combined with Plan A) is not
a particularly effective way to engage him in a discussion
on the topic.

Here are some other maladaptive communication patterns you'd want to avoid:

Sarcasm, which is often totally lost on explosive children (especially the black-and-white thinking variety) because they don't have the skills to figure out that the parent means the exact opposite of what he or she actually says.

Put-downs ("What's the matter with you?! Why can't you be more like your sister?").

Catastrophizing, in which parents greatly exaggerate the effect of current behavior on a child's future well-being ("We've resigned ourselves to the fact that James will probably end up in jail someday").

Interrupting (Don't forget, the child is probably having trouble sorting through his thoughts in the first place. Your interruptions don't help.)

Lecturing ("How many times do I have to tell you . . .").

Dwelling on the past ("Listen, kid, your duck's been upside down in the water for a long time . . . you think I'm gonna get all excited just because you've put together a few good weeks?").

Talking through a third person ("I'm very upset about this, and your father is going to tell you why . . . isn't that right, dear?").

All very counterproductive.

Over time the goal is for you to demonstrate to your child that you can avoid these patterns, anticipate problems before they occur, discuss problems proactively, effectively drill for information, understand his concerns, resist the temptation to dismiss his concerns, articulate your own concerns, and patiently generate and evaluate potential solutions without veering into Plan A or Plan C. This is very hard to do—and worth the effort. There's no shame in having difficulty doing it on your own; seek out a reputable family therapist if you need one.

Speaking of communication patterns, here's what a family session looked like with Mitchell and his parents, whom you first met in chapter 4:

Mitchell and his parents arrived for their second meeting with their new therapist, who was advised that it had been a difficult week.

"We can't talk to him anymore—about anything—without him going crazy," said Mitchell's mother.

"THAT'S NOT SO, MOTHER!" Mitchell boomed. "I'm not going to sit here and listen to you exaggerate."

"Why don't you stand then?" the father cracked.

Mitchell paused, reflecting on his father's words. "If you were joking, then you're even less funny than I thought you were. If you weren't, then you're dumber than I thought you were."

"I'm not the one who flunked out of prep school," the father jabbed back.

"AND I'M NOT THE ONE WHO MADE ME GO TO THAT SCHOOL!" Mitchell boomed.

"Look, I'm really not interested in getting into a pissing contest with you, Mitchell," said the father.

"What do you call what you just did?" the mother chimed in. "Anyway, I don't think Mitchell is ready to face flunking out of prep school yet."

"DON'T SPEAK FOR ME, MOTHER!" Mitchell boomed. "YOU DON'T KNOW WHAT I'M READY TO FACE!"

"Pardon me for interrupting," the therapist said, "but is this the way conversations usually go in this family?"

"Why? Do you think we're all lunatics?" asked Mitchell.

"Speak for yourself," said the father.

"Screw you," said Mitchell.

"Well, we're off to a wonderful start, aren't we?" said the mother.

"WE ARE NOT OFF TO A WONDERFUL START, MOTHER!" Mitchell boomed.

"I was being sarcastic," said the mother. "I thought a little humor might lighten things up a bit."

"I'm not amused," Mitchell grumbled.

"Fortunately, we're not here to amuse you," said the father.

"Sorry to interrupt you folks again," the therapist said. "But I'm still wondering if this is a pretty typical conversation."

"Oh, Mitchell would have gotten insulted and stormed out of the room if we were at home," said the mother. "In fact, I'm surprised he's still sitting here now."

"YOU HAVE NO IDEA HOW I FEEL!" boomed Mitchell.

"We've been listening to you telling us how you feel since

you could talk," said the father. "We know more about how you feel than you know."

"ENOUGH!" boomed Mitchell.

"My sentiments exactly," the therapist said. "I think I'll answer my own question. Forgive me for being so direct, but you guys have some not-so-wonderful ways of communicating with one another."

"How do you mean?" asked the mother.

"You're a very sarcastic group," the therapist said. "Which would be fine, I guess, except that when you're sarcastic, I think it makes it very hard for Mitchell to figure out what you mean."

"But he's so smart and we're so dumb," said the father.

Mitchell paused, reflecting on his father's words. "Are you trying to be funny again?" he asked.

"You're so smart, figure it out," the father said.

"Um," the therapist interrupted, "I'm sure you guys could do this all day, but I don't think it would get us anywhere."

Mitchell chuckled. "He still thinks we're going to accomplish something by coming here."

"I should add that sarcasm isn't the only bad habit," the therapist continued. "The one-upmanship in this family is intense."

"Birds of a feather," the mother chirped.

"What does that mean?" Mitchell demanded.

"It means that the apple didn't fall far from the tree," said the mother.

"Be careful about whose tree you're talking about," said the father. "I don't want any credit for this."

"Oh, I'm afraid you're right in the thick of things," the

therapist reassured the father. "I wonder if we could establish a few rules of communicating. I must warn you, I'm not sure you'll have much to say to one another once I tell you these rules."

"Bravo," said Mitchell. "That's music to my ears."

"What kind of rules?" asked the mother.

"Well, it would be a lot more productive if we got rid of a lot of the sarcasm," the therapist said. "It really muddies up the communication waters. And the one-upmanship has got to go."

The ensuing silence was broken by the father. "I don't think he can do it," he said, looking at Mitchell.

Before Mitchell could erupt, the therapist interjected, "That's one-upmanship."

Mitchell's frown turned upside down. "Thank you," he said.

"This is going to be hard," said the father. "And no more sarcasm either?"

"Not if you guys want your son to start talking to you again," the therapist said.

"Where's that team spirit, fellas?" the mother chimed in.

"That's sarcasm," the therapist interjected.

"Oooh, this guy is tough," said the father, turning to his wife. "I don't like coming here anymore." He smiled.

"That's sarcasm, too," the therapist said.

"My husband isn't accustomed to being corrected," said the mother.

"Oh, that reminds me of the last bad habit," the therapist said.

"Oh, no, what did I say?" the mother said, covering her mouth.

"You guys talk for one another a lot," the therapist said, *"like you can read one another's minds."*

"Well, we know one another very well," said the mother.

"That may be," the therapist said, *"but from what I've observed, your speculations about one another are often off-target, and they don't go over very well."*

"What'd you call it?" asked the mother.

"Speculation," the therapist said. *"Thinking you know what's going on in someone's head. It just gets you guys more agitated with one another."*

"No more speculation?" said the mother.

"Not if you guys want to actually start talking to one another," the therapist confirmed.

"What should we do if someone does one of those three things?" Mitchell asked.

"Just point it out to them without being judgmental," the therapist said. *"If someone is sarcastic, just say, 'That's sarcasm.' If someone is one-upping, say, 'That's one-upmanship.' And if someone is speculating, say . . ."*

' "That's speculation,'" said Mitchell.

"My, we catch on fast," said the father.

"That's sarcasm," said Mitchell.

GRANDPARENTS

At times it's necessary to bring grandparents into the mix. In many families, grandparents or other relatives function as co-parents, taking care of the children while the parents are at work. Even if grandparents don't spend much time with the child—but never miss an opportunity to tell the parents what they would do if they were in charge—they need to be brought into the loop, enlightened about the lagging skills and unsolved problems that set the stage for their grandchild's challenging behavior, and to be helped to understand why the way things were done in the good old days doesn't solve any problems durably or teach any lagging skills.

YOU

This is a restatement of the obvious, but an explosive child can put tremendous pressure on a marriage. In many two-parent families, one parent is primarily disposed toward Plan A and the other is primarily disposed toward Plan C. Since neither approach is working, they have little to show for their disparate predispositions. Yet it's not unusual for the two adults to blame each other for the failure to make much headway on reducing explosions:

Parent #1: If you'd just let me deal with him and stop letting him off the hook, things would be different around here!

Parent #2: I'm not going to stand by and watch you screaming at him and punishing him all the time. Somebody needs to give the kid a break!

Troubles between a couple can make life with an explosive child much more difficult. Some partners aren't even very good at collaboratively solving problems with each other, so working on unsolved problems with a child can require new skills. Partners who are drained by their own difficulties often have little left for a labor-intensive explosive child. Sometimes one partner feels exhausted and resentful that he or she has to be the primary parent because the other parent spends a lot of time at work.

It's hard to work on helping your child if you're feeling the need to put your own house in order first. Some parents find that they're lacking some of the same skills that their explosive child is lacking. (Plan B ought to help them both learn new skills.) For one mother, her son's explosions tapped into her own abusive childhood, and it was extremely difficult for her to get past her visceral reaction to her son's raised voice.

Mother: I'm not using Plan A. I'm not going to do to him what my parents did to me.

Therapist: Okay.

Mother: But I don't want him walking all over me— that's what my parents did to me—so I'm not using Plan C.

Therapist: Okay.

Mother: So what should I do?

Therapist: Use Plan B.

Another mother felt so drained by being a single parent to her three other children that she simply had no energy left for helping her explosive son. Many parents are quite bitter about having been dealt an explosive hand by the great deck shuffler of children. One father had to get a handle on his own explosiveness before he could help his daughter with hers. He found that many of the Plan B strategies he was using with his daughter helped him explode less often, too. Another father needed to be medicated for ADHD before he was able to stick to the plan agreed on in treatment. Yet another father had to come to grips with his excessive drinking and its impact on the whole family before he could press ahead with Plan B. Take care of yourself. Work hard at creating a support system for yourself. Seek professional help or other forms of support if you need it. These things don't change on their own.

Q & A

Question: My spouse won't use Plan B. He won't even read this book. Any advice?

Answer: For some adults, books are not the best way to access new information. Maybe your spouse will listen to a CD in the car? Or access information on a Web site? You'll want to check out www.explosivechild .com for lots of potential resources. But there are also a lot of adults out there who fear that their concerns won't be heard or addressed, so they head straight for Plan A when they have a concern. Why are there a lot of adults who fear that their concerns won't be heard or addressed? Because there are a lot of adults who were raised with Plan A as children and their concerns were neither heard nor addressed! Adults who are perpetuating the cycle by using Plan A often need to be reminded that their concerns will be heard and addressed with Plan B as well. Then they need to practice Plan B so they can get good at it.

Question: But my husband says Plan A worked for him.

Answer: It depends on what he means by "worked." You can get away with Plan A with a kid who has the skills to handle imposition of adult will adaptively. But your kid apparently doesn't have those skills. (If he did, he wouldn't be exploding whenever you impose your will.). If Plan A is simply causing explosions and hostility and misery, then it's hard to imagine why your husband would want to stick with something that's not working. Maybe he thinks his only other option is Plan C. We'll have to help him learn about that third option.

Question: I've been taught that it's important for parents to be consistent with each other in front of the child so the child can't do any "splitting." So what advice do you give parents if one is using Plan A on an issue and the other disagrees?

Answer: Explosions are far more destructive to families than parents disagreeing in front of their children. If two parents agree that an unsolved problem should be pursued with their child, then *they already agree on the main point.* If one parent is pursuing the unsolved problem with Plan A, causing an explosion, teaching no skills, and failing to solve the problem durably, then good teamwork would have the other parent intercede to pursue the unsolved problem with Plan B instead. Life is a bit more interesting if one parent is intent on using Plan A to deal with an unsolved problem and the other is using Plan C, for this suggests that the parents are not yet in agreement about whether the unsolved problem should be pursued. In this case, the parents need to revisit their list of unsolved problems to achieve a consensus on which unsolved problems are to be resolved (through Plan B) and which are to be dropped for now (that's Plan C).

Question: My explosive child has siblings who are nonexplosive and respond well to Plan A. Am I supposed to have two different types of discipline going on in my household at the same time?

Answer: Kids who respond to Plan A tend to respond to Plan B as well, so if you're determined to be consistent, use Plan B with your nonexplosive kids, too. But here's another angle: as you've read, there isn't a household in the world where all the children are treated exactly the same. In all households, one child is getting something another isn't getting. Again, fair does not mean equal. Your nonexplosive children want your explosive child to stop exploding more than they want everyone to be treated exactly the same.

11

The Dinosaur in the Building

As hard as it is to help an explosive child within a family, it may be even harder in a school. After all, there are twenty or thirty other students in the child's classes, many with a wide range of special needs. Like parents, most general education teachers and school administrators haven't received any specialized training to help them understand and assist an explosive child. There are a lot of different people to get onto the same page. And there's a big dinosaur in the building: the existing school discipline program.

Fortunately, most explosive kids don't explode at school. This reality often reinforces the false belief that a kid's explosions are intentional, goal-oriented, and completely under his control. Here are a few alternative explanations for the home-school disparity:

- *The situational factor:* As you've read, explosions occur when the demands of the environment exceed a kid's capacity to respond well. For some explosive kids, the demands of the school environment don't exceed their capacity to respond well, but certain demands of the home environment do. For example, because the school environment tends to be relatively structured and predictable, it can actually be more "user-friendly" for some explosive kids than the home environment. As you'd imagine, there are explosive kids who don't find the structure and predictability of school to be user-friendly at all; they're often the ones who explode at school, too.

- *The embarrassment factor:* Many explosive kids would be absolutely mortified if their classmates and teachers witnessed an explosive episode, so they put massive amounts of energy into holding it together at school. But since the embarrassment factor can't be replicated at home, and since the energy can't be maintained 24–7, the kid unravels the minute he gets home. Most of us are better behaved outside the home than we are inside, so explosive kids aren't especially unusual in this regard. And, of course, there are explosive kids whose frustration at school blows right through the embarrassment factor.

- *The chemical factor:* Teachers and classmates are often the primary beneficiaries of pharmacotherapy, but many medications wear off by late afternoon or early evening, just in time for explosions at home.

The fact that a kid isn't exploding at school doesn't mean that school isn't contributing to explosions that occur elsewhere. Lots of things can happen at school to fuel explosions outside of school: being teased by other kids, feeling socially isolated or rejected, feeling frustrated and embarrassed over struggles on certain academic tasks, feeling misunderstood by the teacher. Homework, of course, often extends academic frustrations well beyond the end of the school day. So schools still have a role to play in helping, even if they don't see the kid at his worst.

But this chapter is primarily focused on the kids who do explode at school. You may recall that Casey, one of the children you read about in chapters 4 and 8, had a pattern of running out of the classroom when he became frustrated by a challenging academic task or difficult interaction with a peer. When he wasn't running out of the room, he was exploding in the room, turning red, crying, screaming, crumpling paper, breaking pencils, falling on the floor, and refusing to work. Danny, another of the children you read about in chapters 4 and 8, was also prone to the occasional explosion at school. On one particularly memorable day, the teacher designated him to hand out doughnuts to his classmates after recess. Following recess, he hurried back to the classroom to hand out the doughnuts, but a parent who had volunteered to help out that day was already in the room and insisted on being the doughnut distributor. Danny attempted to explain to the parent that he had been assigned the task of giving out the doughnuts, but the parent, trying to be helpful, insisted on doing it. The shift in Danny's thinking demanded by this case of reciprocal inflexibility was more than Danny could handle. *Kaboom.*

Luckily, the CPS model is as applicable to schools and classrooms as it is to homes and families. But implementation at school isn't easy. We live in the era of inclusion (by the way, that's a good thing), which has placed many students with special behavioral and academic needs in mainstream classrooms, thereby providing these students with opportunities to interact with "ordinary" kids (and vice versa) and reducing the stigma of having special needs addressed only outside of the classroom. While every student in a given classroom needs something special, a typical mainstream classroom is now likely to have numerous students officially designated as having "special needs," some with disorders their teachers have never worked with before. In many instances teachers justifiably feel that they lack the expertise and are not being provided with the kind of support they need to understand and help kids with social, emotional, and behavioral challenges.

To make matters worse, we in the United States also live in the era of high-stakes testing, which places teachers in the position of trying to make sure that every square peg fits into the round holes defined by academic standards for different grades. My sense is that such testing has made it even harder for some teachers to maintain the proper perspective and devote the necessary attention and energy to students who exhibit challenging behavior. What a shame, since challenging behavior deserves the same compassion and effort as any other developmental delay.

And to make things still worse, the zero-tolerance policies that have been driving discipline programs in many schools tend to be a road map (sometimes called a *rubric*) for Plan A. Such programs are usually comprised of a list (often a long one) of things students shouldn't do and a list (often a long one) of what's going to happen if they do them. But standard school disciplinary practices often aren't terribly effective for the students to whom they are most frequently applied, and aren't needed for the students to whom they are never applied. The school discipline program isn't the reason well-behaved students behave well. They behave well *because they can*. And we have little good to show for the millions of punishments—detentions, suspensions, expulsions—that are meted out every year to the kids who are having difficulty handling the social, emotional, and behavioral expectations at school. And yet most administrators' standard rationale for the continued use of consequences goes something like this:

We have to set an example for all our students; even if sus-pension doesn't help Casey, at least it sets an example for our other students. We need to let them know that we take safety seriously at our school.

Time for a few questions.

Question: What message do we give the other students if we continue to apply interventions that aren't helping Casey behave more adaptively?

Answer: That we're actually not sure how to help explosive kids behave more adaptively.

Question: What's the likelihood that the students who aren't explosive would become explosive if we did not make an example of Casey?

Answer: As a general rule, slim to none.

Question: What message do we give Casey if we continue to apply strategies that aren't working?

Answer: "We don't understand you and we can't help you."

Question: Under which circumstance do we have the best chance of helping Casey learn and practice better ways of dealing with his inflexibility and low frustration tolerance: when he's in school or when he's suspended from school?

Answer: In school.

Question: Why do many schools continue to use interventions that aren't working for their explosive students?

Answer: They aren't sure what else to do.

Question: What happens to students to whom these interventions are counterproductively applied for many years?

Answer: They become more alienated and fall farther outside the social fabric of the school.

Question: Isn't it the parents' job to make their child behave at school?

Answer: Helping a child deal more adaptively with frustration is everyone's job. Besides, the parents aren't there when the child is exploding at school.

Question: Isn't it the job of special education to handle these children?

Answer: Actually, special education often has very little to offer many explosive students.

Time for Plan B. But implementing the CPS model in a school is no small undertaking. Here are some of the necessary components:

Awareness: Kids with social, emotional, and behavioral challenges are being ill served by current school disciplinary practices in many schools. Some educators know this already and are eager to learn new ways of understanding and helping these kids. Other educators still don't know this and need to be enlightened.

Urgency: Understanding and helping these kids has to be a priority. However, since educators have so many different competing priorities, making explosive students a priority could be a problem. But we're losing a lot of kids unnecessarily because their behavioral challenges are misunderstood and mishandled.

Mentality: An adult's mentality or philosophy about children is what guides and governs his or her response when a student is not doing well. Many schools have adopted the *kids do well if they can* mentality and are therefore spending a lot less time "teaching kids who's boss" or seeking ways to give kids the incentive to do well.

Expertise: Many educators apply to explosive students the same principles and practices of discipline that were effective with their own children, and the results are often poor. Other educators believe that the expertise necessary for understanding and helping an explosive child is well beyond their grasp. Not true. Educators need expertise and experience in identifying lagging skills and unsolved problems and in using Plan B. The expertise comes from reading books like this one. The experience comes from practice which, first and foremost, requires effort and courage. Proficiency comes after that.

Time: Classroom teachers often feel that they don't have time to help kids with social, emotional, and behavioral challenges. But while Plan B does take time, it also saves time. That's because doing the right thing and fixing the problem always takes less time than doing the wrong thing and not fixing the problem. Before teachers and administrators embrace and learn how to use Plan B, time is usually a major concern. But concerns about time fade once educators make it a priority to understand and help these kids, become skilled at Plan B, and embrace its use. There are some natural times built into the school day—before and after school, during lunch, during recess, prep time, while the other kids are working on an assignment—for using Proactive Plan B with an explosive student, and I've yet to meet the administrator who isn't willing to arrange for coverage so that a classroom teacher can use Proactive Plan B with an individual student. Some schools have found it worthwhile to retool the entire schedule to create the time needed for helping kids who would otherwise become lost in the shuffle.

Assessment Mechanisms and Tools: It will be necessary to achieve a consensus on the lagging skills and unsolved problems of each explosive student so that the factors underlying his difficulties are well understood and the events that reliably precipitate his explosions are clear. So often I've seen school personnel blame a kid's parents for the difficulties he's having at school or "explain" the kid's difficulties by reciting his diagnoses. As you now know, diagnoses don't really explain much of anything. And, in the same way that parents of well-behaved kids get more credit than they deserve for their kids' desirable behavior, parents of explosive kids get more blame than they deserve for their kids' undesirable behavior. Blaming parents is a dead end, and it makes it much harder to focus on the things school personnel could actually do something about: unsolved problems and lagging skills.

Identifying lagging skills and unsolved problems usually requires a meeting or two involving all of the adults who interact with the child at school. It often makes sense to have parents and relevant mental health professionals involved in the process as well. If interventions occur before the "interveners" have a clear sense of what they're working on, the interventions are likely to be ineffective. An important facet of this step is to identify the two or three unsolved problems that are to be the focal points of initial Plan B discussions, then to determine the specific adults who will be using Plan B with the student on each problem.

I've developed an instrument called the Assessment of Lagging Skills and Unsolved Problems (ALSUP) to assist in the process. It's a list of the lagging skills described in chapter 3, along with various unsolved problems, and can be found at www.explosivechild.com. Many schools have incorporated the ALSUP into their functional assessments. And if it's necessary to quantify a kid's difficulties or progress, the ALSUP is available in a Likert-scale format.

Practice, Feedback, and Coaching: Once mechanisms for assessment are in place, schools are ready for the next step: becoming proficient at Plan B. For most people, this is a process that will require practice and ongoing feedback and coaching. This can take a variety of forms in different schools, and a variety of resources are available for support (details, once again, are at www.explosivechild. com). Certain aspects of Plan B tend to be quite challenging for many adults, including educators: "drilling" for information in the Empathy step; identifying and articulating one's concern or perspective; hanging in there while different solutions are generated and considered. After numerous attempts, adults come to recognize their own unique vulnerabilities in using Plan B. For example, many stumble in their use of Plan B because of pre-conceived notions about kids' concerns, which can make it very difficult to drill for information in an unbiased fashion. Other adults are inclined toward preordained solutions, which can make it hard to explore the range of mutually satisfactory and realistic possibilities.

Communication: Because Proactive Plan B is far preferable to Emergency Plan B, advance preparation and good communication among adults are essential. The only models for treatment that don't require good communication are the *ineffective* ones. To help out, another instrument—called the Plan B Flowchart—can be found at www.explosivechild.com as well. It was designed to help adults keep track of the different unsolved problems that are precipitating explosions in an individual kid. I've found that, in schools as well as in homes, there's a tendency to work on the "hot" problem that precipitated an explosion on a certain day. But since unsolved problems wax and wane, the "hot" unsolved problem that was addressed one day or week (but not seen through to a final resolution) is often replaced the next day or week by a different "hot" unsolved problem. However, the first unsolved problem hasn't gone away, it's just gone into "hibernation." Since it's still unsolved; it's coming back. The Plan B Flowchart is designed to prevent that from happening by helping adults track unsolved problems over time until they're durably resolved. As you'd imagine, the need for ongoing monitoring means that the adults who are working with a given child will have to reconvene periodically to assess progress and revisit unsolved problems.

Perseverance: Show me an explosive kid who people are trying to fix quickly and I'll show you an explosive kid it's taking a very long time to fix. There is no quick fix. You're in this for the long haul. You don't fix a reading disability in a week, and you don't fix this developmental delay in a week either. There will be bumps in the road. Transforming school discipline is a project. It doesn't happen overnight. But it needs to happen.

Naturally, there's much more that could be said about each of these components. That's why I wrote *Lost at School*, which was published in 2008.

This might be a good time to point out that Plan B isn't limited to adult–child problem solving. The ingredients of Plan B are equally applicable to unsolved problems between two students as well as to those that affect an entire group of students. And Plan B has significant ramifications for adult–adult problem solving as well. For the remainder of this chapter, let's see what Plan B would look like as applied to these different types of problem solving in a school setting. We'll start with Plan B involving a teacher and student, move on to Plan B between students, and finish with parents and teachers.

STUDENT–TEACHER PROBLEM SOLVING

As you'll see, Proactive Plan B doesn't really look much different when the adult is a teacher from the way it looks when the adult is a parent. The ingredients are exactly the same, though the topics may differ. Here's an example between a teacher and a thirteen-year-old:

Teacher: Class, please get to work on your social studies projects.

Rickey: I'm not doing it.

Teacher: Well, then your grade will reflect both your attitude and your lack of effort.

Rickey: I don't give a damn about my grades. I can't do this crap.

Teacher: Your mouth just bought you a detention, young man. And I don't want students in my classroom who don't do their work. Anything else you'd like to say?

Rickey: Yeah, this class sucks.

Teacher: Nor do I need to listen to this. You need to go to the assistant principal's office NOW.

Oops. That was Plan A, wasn't it? Tricky author. Since this was apparently an emergent problem, the teacher has much better options: "momentary" Plan C or Emergency Plan B. Here's what momentary Plan C would look like:

Teacher: Class, please get to work on your social studies projects.

Rickey: I'm not doing it.

Teacher: Is there something about the assignment that's hard for you? Let's see if we can figure it out.

Rickey: Forget it. I can't do this! Just leave me alone! Damn!

Teacher: Rickey, can you just hang for a second? Let me get everyone else going, and then you and I can figure out what's the matter and see what we can do about it.

And here's what the same problem would look like if it were handled with Emergency Plan B:

Teacher: Class, please get to work on your social studies projects.

Rickey: I'm not doing it.

Teacher: Is there something about the assignment that's hard for you? Let's see if we can figure it out.

Rickey: Forget it. I can't do this! Just leave me alone! Damn!

Teacher: Rickey, listen a second. I know you have trouble with writing and spelling, and you get very frustrated when you have to do assignments where you have to write and spell. Let's see if we can find a way for you to do the important part of the assignment—letting me know what you thought of the story you just heard, which is something you're very good at—without your getting all frustrated about the writing and spelling part.

Rickey: How?

Teacher: Well, maybe Darren would help you write down your thoughts. You could sort of dictate your thoughts to him.

Rickey: No way.

Teacher: How come?

Rickey: He's going to give me a hard time about needing his help.

Teacher: Hmm. Is there anyone who could help you who wouldn't give you a hard time about it?

Rickey: DeJuan.

Teacher: DeJuan? That could work. You'd feel more comfortable with him?

Rickey: Yeah, he's smart.

Teacher: You're smart, too. You just have some trouble with writing and spelling.

It's important to note that while momentary Plan C and Emergency Plan B are useful for defusing eruptions, Rickey's writing and spelling problems are *predictable*. So rather than using momentary Plan C or Emergency B on a daily basis—which is very time-consuming—the teacher would want to schedule a time to work on the problem with Rickey using Proactive Plan B, preferably before the problem erupts again in the middle of another lesson.

By the way, the ingredients of Plan B can be applied to every student in the class, each of whom has problems that need to be solved. If every student is working on something, then the explosive kid doesn't stick out like a sore thumb—you're using Plan B with everyone.

STUDENT–STUDENT AND GROUP
PROBLEM SOLVING

Plan B can also be applied to unsolved problems that may arise between two students. In such instances, the teacher's role is Plan B facilitator. Here's an example from *Lost at School*:

Mr. Bartlett: Zach, as you know, in our classroom when something is bothering somebody we try to talk about it. As I mentioned to you yesterday, I thought it might be a good idea for me and you and Anna to talk together about the project you guys are supposed to be doing together.

Zach: Okay.

Mr. Bartlett: She has some concerns about what it's going to be like doing the project with you. It sounds like you guys worked on a project together last year, yes?

Zach: Yup.

Mr. Bartlett: I don't know if you knew this, but Anna came away from that project feeling like you weren't very receptive to her ideas and feeling like she did most of the work. So she wasn't too sure she wanted to do this project with you.

Zach: She doesn't have to do the project with me. I can find another partner.

Mr. Bartlett: Yes, she was thinking the same thing. But I was hoping we could find a way for you guys to work well together. What do you think of Anna's concern?

Zach: I don't know. That was a long time ago.

Mr. Bartlett: Do you remember how you guys figured out what to do on last year's project?

Zach: No.

Mr. Bartlett: Do you remember Anna's doing most of the work?

Zach: Sort of. But that's because she didn't like the way I was doing it, so she decided to do it herself.

Anna: That is so not true. I did most of the work because you wouldn't do anything.

Zach: Well, that's not how I remember it.

Mr. Bartlett: It sounds like you both have different recollections about what happened last year and why it didn't go so well, so maybe we shouldn't concentrate so much on what happened last year. I don't know if you would ever agree on that. Maybe we should focus on the concerns that are getting in the way of your working together this year. Anna, your concern is that Zach won't listen to any of your ideas. And you're both concerned about the possibility that Anna will do all the work. I wonder if there's a way for you guys to make sure that you have equal input into the design of the project, without having Anna do all the work in the end. Do you guys have any ideas?

Anna: This is so pointless. He won't listen to my ideas.

Mr. Bartlett: Well, I know that's what you feel happened last year, but I can't do anything about last year. We're trying to focus on this year and on coming up with a solution so that you and Zach have equal input and work equally hard.

Anna: Can you sit with us while we're figuring out what to do? Then you'll see what I mean.

Zach: Then you'll see what I mean.

Mr. Bartlett: So, Anna, you're saying that maybe if I sit in on your discussions I might be able to help you guys have a more equal exchange of ideas?

Anna: That's not really what I meant.

Mr. Bartlett: I know . . . but I'm thinking that it might not be a bad way to ensure the equal exchange of ideas. What do you think?

Zach: I think we can work together.

Anna: Fine, sit in on our discussion and help us have equal input.

Mr. Bartlett: Only if that works for you guys.

Anna: It only works for me if I have to work with him.

Mr. Bartlett: I'm not saying you have to work with him. I'm saying I'd like you to give it a shot so the other kids don't have to break up their pairs. We can entertain other options if that solution doesn't work for you.

Anna: What other solutions?

Mr. Bartlett: I don't know. Whatever we come up with. Can you guys think of any others?

Zach: We could do the project by ourselves, you

know, alone. She could do one and I could do one.

Mr. Bartlett: Well, that would probably work for you guys, but it wouldn't work for me. One of the goals of this project was for kids to learn to work together. I think it's an important skill.

Anna: Why don't we try to work together, with you helping us, and if that doesn't work we can do our own projects.

Mr. Bartlett: Zach, does that solution work for you?

Zach: Sure, whatever.

Mr. Bartlett: I need to think about whether it works for me. You guys'll try hard to work together with me helping you?

Anna: Yes.

Zach: Yes.

Mr. Bartlett: Okay, let's go with it. We're working on the project again tomorrow. I'll sit in on your discussion with each other and see if I can help make sure the exchange of ideas is equal and the workload is equal. Let's see how it goes.

While some problems are best addressed by using Plan B with individual students or pairs of students, other problems—especially those that affect the group as a whole—are best addressed by using Plan B with the entire classroom community. Group discussions are a common occurrence in many classrooms, but mostly on topics that have an academic orientation and a right or wrong answer. But when Plan B is added to a group discussion, and when such discussions are about nonacademic problems such as bullying, teasing, and general classroom conduct, then community members learn to listen to and take into account each other's concerns and recognize that there are no "right" answers, only solutions that are mutually satisfactory. Group problem solving is very hard, but no harder and messier than having problems that never get solved or having problems that "go underground" because there is no mechanism for solving them.

Yet again, the ingredients are the same, and the classroom teacher is the facilitator. The first goal is to achieve the clearest possible understanding of the concerns and perspectives of each group member with regard to a given problem. Once the concerns have been well clarified, the group moves on to the next challenge: finding a solution that will address those concerns. The criteria for an ingenious solution remain the same: it must be realistic and mutually satisfactory.

In group Plan B, the teacher helps the group decide what problems to tackle first, keeps the group focused and serious (group members will eventually take on these responsibilities as well), and ensures that the exploration of concerns and solutions is exhaustive. The teacher's stance in helping the group sort through concerns and solutions is generally *neutral*. There are no good or bad concerns, no such thing as "competing" concerns, only concerns that need to be addressed. Likewise, there are no right or wrong solutions, only ones that are realistic (or not) and mutually satisfactory (or not).

PARENT–TEACHER PROBLEM SOLVING

Parents of explosive kids and school personnel often have difficulty working together for the same reasons that kids and adults do: the tendency to blame one party or another; the failure to achieve a consensus on the true nature of a kid's difficulties (lagging skills) and the true events (unsolved problems) precipitating explosions; the failure to identify the concerns of the respective parties; and the attempt of one party to impose its will on another. As Sarah Lawrence-Lightfoot writes in her insightful book *The Essential Conversation: What Parents and Teachers Can Learn from Each Other*, great potential exists for productive collaboration between parents and teachers. When parents and teachers are able to exchange highly specific information about a child's lagging skills and unsolved problems, they start trusting each other. Parents become convinced that they are being heard and that the teacher sees, knows, and cares about their child. Educators become convinced that the parents are eager for information, eager to collaborate, and eager to help in any way possible. Both parties need to be part of the process of working toward a mutually satisfactory action plan. You're on the same team.

Here's what Proactive Plan B looks like between parents and teachers. Once again, it uses the same ingredients: information gathering and understanding, entering the concerns of both parties into consideration, and brainstorming solutions that are realistic and mutually satisfactory.

Teacher: I understand that homework has been very difficult lately.

Mother: Homework has been very difficult for a very long time. You're the first teacher Rickey's had who's expressed any interest in what we go through with homework. We spend several hours fighting over homework every weeknight and every weekend.

Teacher: I'm sorry about that. But let's see if we can figure out what's so hard about homework and then come up with a plan so it's not so terrible anymore.

Mother: You can't imagine how nice that would be.

Teacher: Can you tell me the parts of homework that have been difficult for you and Rickey? Or is it all hard? You don't mind if I write these down, do you?

Mother: Not at all. He's a very slow writer. So he gets frustrated that homework takes as long as it does. And he seems to have trouble thinking of a lot of the details you're asking for. And he's always struggled with spelling. Last year's teacher told us not to worry about the spelling. But Rickey doesn't seem to be able to do that. So I don't know whether to forget about it or work on it. I wouldn't know how to work on it anyway! And I end up doing a lot of the writing for him.

Teacher: Yes, I've noticed the slow writing part, and the difficulty he has coming up with details, and his troubles with spelling. How about math?

Mother: He breezes right through it. Very little writing, very little spelling, and not the kind of details he has trouble with.

Teacher: Well, then, let's take our problems one at a time. Of course I've only had Rickey in my class for about four weeks now, so I can't say I have a perfect handle on his difficulties or what we should do about them. And I have begun working with Rickey on these problems myself, so I'm in the midst of trying to gather some information from him, too. But I'm not one for having kids spend two hours on homework every night, and I'm certainly not one for having homework cause problems between kids and their parents. Of course, I'm not always aware that those problems exist, so I appreciate your honesty.

Mother: I'm not shy about letting people know what's going on with Rickey. I just wish we were seeing more progress on the problems he's having.

Teacher: The thing is, we're going to need to get Rickey involved in the homework discussion, too. Even if you and I come up with brilliant solutions, they won't be so brilliant if he's not on board with them. So maybe we should use this discussion to make sure we have a clear sense of the problems we need to get solved. One problem is the amount of time homework is consuming. Yes?

Mother: Yes!

Teacher: But it sounds like a lot of that time is spent being frustrated over what to work on and how you can help, so that's something we'll need to get solved, too.

Mother: Absolutely.

Teacher: I'm not convinced that Rickey can't get better at spelling, so I'm disinclined to tell you that we should drop it altogether. Plus, as you said, Rickey doesn't seem able to drop it. So spelling is an unsolved problem. And slow writing is an unsolved problem. And fleshing out the details is an unsolved problem. And I know you're doing a lot of the writing for him, but we don't want him getting the idea that he doesn't need to do any of the writing.

Mother: Aren't you overwhelmed by all this?

Teacher: No, I actually find that sorting through unsolved problems helps me be less overwhelmed. At least I know what needs to be addressed.

Mother: I see what you mean.

Teacher: Any other unsolved problems related to homework?

Mother: Well, he has hockey practice two nights a week, so sometimes he's really tired when it's time for homework. Those are our really tough nights.

Teacher: I can imagine. So we have some work to do, don't we?

Mother: It appears so.

Teacher: Here's what I'm thinking. If it's okay with you, why don't we meet again within the next week, but next time let's include Rickey in the meeting. Then we can start talking about how these problems can be solved, one at a time

What's the solution to the writing problem? The spelling problem? The details problem? The hockey practice problem? That's for Rickey, his mom, and his teacher to figure out. There are dozens of possibilities. There's no such thing as a "right" or "wrong" solution—only solutions that are realistic, mutually satisfactory, and durable. What will they do if the first solution to a given problem doesn't stand the test of time? They'll head back to Plan B, figure out what didn't work—in other words, what it was about the solution that wasn't realistic and mutually satisfactory—and come up with a better solution.

Q & A

Question: In one of the examples above, you referred to something you called "momentary" Plan C. That suggests there's more than one form of Plan C. Can you elaborate?

Answer: It's not a major point of emphasis, since I'd really rather that people focus more intently on the distinction between Emergency Plan B and Proactive Plan B. But in the example involving Rickey and his refusal to work on his social studies project, "momentary" Plan C was his teacher's device for buying time in anticipation of fairly immediate follow-up with Plan B. A proactive version of Plan C would involve removing an expectation completely for the foreseeable future. So if Rickey's teacher intended to completely eliminate the expectation that Rickey write or spell—at least for the time being—then that would be an example of an unsolved problem that was being handled with "Proactive" Plan C.

Question: I'm a teacher, and I'm a little worried about having different sets of expectations for different kids. If I let one kid get away with something, won't my other students try to get away with it as well?

Answer: Plan B isn't about letting students get away with something. And teachers usually have different expectations for different children already. That's why some students receive special reading help while others do not; why some students are in a gifted program for math while others are not. If a student asks why one of his classmates is being treated differently, the classroom teacher has the perfect opportunity to do some educating: "Everyone in our classroom gets what he or she needs. If someone needs help with something, we all try to help him or her. And everyone in our class needs something special." It's no different when a child needs help with flexibility, frustration tolerance, and problem solving. Here's how that looked with Casey:

"We can't let Casey keep running out of the room," the school principal said gravely. "It's dangerous, and we're responsible for his safety."

It was March of Casey's first-grade year, and the principal was presiding over a meeting that included Casey's teacher, occupational therapist, guidance counselor, special education coordinator, parents, and psychologist. Casey was blowing up a lot less often at home, but there were still some kinks to work out at school.

"Well," the psychologist said, "as you know, in some ways Casey's leaving the classroom is more adaptive than some of the other things he could be doing in response to frustration—like tearing the room apart. But I agree, it's very important that he stay safe."

"What's making Casey act this way?" asked the classroom teacher. "What's his diagnosis?"

"Well, I don't think a diagnosis will tell us much about why he's acting this way. But I think it's safe to say he's having a lot of trouble shifting from one mind-set to another and that he's not very good at solving problems," the psychologist said.

"So why does he run out of the room?" asked the teacher.

"Because he can't think of anything else to do," the psychologist said. "I think we need to start solving some of the problems that are causing Casey to get so frustrated that he can't think of anything to do but run out of the room. But he may not stop

running out of the room completely yet. We may need a place where he can go to settle down when he does feel overwhelmed, so he doesn't end up in the parking lot."

The special education coordinator chimed in. "I think we should have consequences if he leaves the classroom," she said. "I don't think it's good for the other kids to see him leave when he gets frustrated."

"Why? Have any of the other kids expressed a desire or shown an inclination to leave the classroom when they're frustrated?" the psychologist asked.

"No," said the teacher.

"Do we think Casey is leaving the classroom because he'd rather be out in the hallway all by himself?" the psychologist asked.

"I don't think so," said the teacher. "He's always very eager to come back in as soon as he's settled down."

"Do we think that punishing him after he leaves the classroom will have any effect on his behavior the next time he's frustrated and feels the need to leave the classroom?" the psychologist asked.

"I don't know," said the teacher. "It's almost as if he's in a completely different zone when he's frustrated."

"Then I'm not certain why we'd punish Casey for leaving the classroom," the psychologist continued. "Especially if the main reason we're doing it is to set an example for the other kids."

"So what do you suggest we do when he gets frustrated?" asked the special education coordinator.

"I think most of our energy should be focused on what to

do before Casey gets frustrated, not after," the psychologist said. "When Casey's frustration with a particular task or situation is predictable, we can solve the problem that's routinely frustrating him ahead of time so he won't get to the point where he needs to run out of the classroom. If we should happen to run into an unpredictable frustration, I think we need a place for Casey to go to calm down if your initial efforts to calm him down don't do the trick. I don't think he's at the point yet where he's able to talk things through once he's frustrated, although we're working on it. Luckily, he's pretty good at calming down on his own if we leave him alone for a while. We have to find ways to let him do that while still making sure he's safe. So for now, our top priority is to keep explosions to a minimum, even at the expense of his learning. It's the explosions that are getting in the way of Casey's learning anyway."

Things went quite well for Casey for the last few months of that school year. At the beginning of the next school year, the group reassembled (including his old and new teachers), reviewed what worked and what didn't the previous school year, and agreed to try to do more of the same, while focusing on helping Casey complete more schoolwork. Although everyone expected some rough moments as Casey adjusted to his new teachers and classmates, it wasn't until two months into the school year that he had his first series of explosions. The special education coordinator hastily called a meeting.

"We think Casey has regressed," the principal said. "He looks as bad as he did last school year."

"Actually, we think he looks a lot better than he did last school year," said Casey's father. "In fact, we were happy he started off as well as he did. He was really looking forward to going back to school."

"I think we need to revisit the idea of consequences," said the special education coordinator. "Do you folks say anything to him about this behavior at home?" she asked the parents.

"Of course we do!" said the mother, a little offended. "We let him know very clearly that it is unacceptable, and he gets very upset because he knows that already. Believe me, this is being addressed at home."

"Is he exploding a lot at home?" asked the principal.

"We haven't had a major explosion in months," said the father. "We'd almost forgotten how bad things used to be."

"I still think Casey needs to know that at school, life doesn't just go on like nothing happened after he has an explosion," said the principal.

"I agree," said the special education coordinator.

"What did you have in mind?" asked the father.

"I think after he blows up, he needs to sit in my office and talk it over," said the principal. "And until he does, he shouldn't be permitted to rejoin his classmates."

"I don't think he's ready for that yet," the father said.

"Well," said the special education coordinator "whether he's ready or not, it's important that the other students see that we disapprove of Casey's behavior."

"His classmates don't already know you disapprove of his behavior?" the psychologist asked.

"We think we need to send a stronger message," the special education coordinator said. "We think he can control this behavior."

"I think we should enforce consequences only if we believe that they will help Casey control himself the next time he gets frustrated," the psychologist said. "Otherwise, consequences are only likely to make him more frustrated."

"We have to do what we think is right in our school," said the principal, ending the discussion.

Casey had a minor explosion two weeks later. He was escorted to the principal's office. The principal tried hard to get Casey to talk about his frustration. Casey couldn't. The principal insisted, setting the stage for a massive, one-hour explosion that included spitting, swearing, and destroying property in the principal's office. Another meeting was hastily called.

"I've never been treated that way by a student!" said the principal. "Casey's going to have to understand that we can't accept that kind of behavior."

"Casey already knows that behavior is unacceptable!" said the mother. "Sometimes he can talk about what's frustrating him right away—and that's a recent development—but most of the time he can't talk about it until much later, and then we have to give him some time to collect himself before we try to help him."

"I tried that," said the principal. "When he was in my office, I told him that I wasn't going to talk to him until he was good and ready."

"How did he respond to that?" the psychologist asked.

"That's when he spit on me," said the principal.

"I guess that tells you that something about what you

said made him more frustrated, not less," the psychologist said.

"You don't think having him sit in my office will eventually help?" asked the principal. "I'm very uncomfortable having him blow up and then watch him go happily out to recess and rejoin the other kids without there being some kind of consequence. I'm struggling with this."

"I think sitting in your office would work great if Casey experienced it as a place where he could calm down rather than as a place where he's asked to do something he can't do yet—namely, talk about things immediately—or where he feels he's being punished for something he already knows he shouldn't have done."

"So why doesn't he just tell me he knows his behavior is unacceptable?" asked the principal.

"I don't think Casey can figure out why he behaves in a way he knows is unacceptable," interjected the father. "After this recent episode, he was very upset. That night he practically begged me to give him more medicine so he wouldn't act that way anymore."

The assembled adults were silent for a brief moment.

"But I can't give the other children in his class the idea that they can do what he does and get away with it," said the principal.

"I honestly don't think that the students who are flexible and handle frustration well are going to start exploding just because they see Casey getting away with it," said the psychologist. "And he's not getting away with it. If you're teaching Casey how to deal more adaptively with frustration and solving the problems that cause him to explode, his class-

mates see that you take his explosions seriously, that you expect him not to explode, and that you know what you're doing. They won't think you know what you're doing if you make things worse."

Did Casey run out of the classroom again during the school year? Yes—to a designated desk in the hallway that he knew was his "chill-out" area. Did he begin returning to the classroom much more rapidly after he left? Absolutely. Did he hit his principal again? No. Did he hit his classmates a few times? Yes—just like many of the other boys in his class. Did he continue to have trouble shifting gears? Yes, sometimes. But his teacher demonstrated to Casey that she could help him when he became frustrated, and Casey thrived in her class. One day I asked the teacher, "Do you think Casey's difficulties affect his relations with his peers?" She replied, "Oh, I think he's well liked despite his difficulties. I think the other kids can tell when Casey's having a rough day, and they try to help him make it through."

Question: Does Plan B undermine a teacher's authority with the other kids in the class?

Answer: No, it doesn't. The other kids are watching closely. If a teacher intervenes in a way that solves problems, teaches skills, and reduces the likelihood of an explosion, he or she has done nothing to undermine his or her authority with the other kids.

Question: Is it really fair to expect teachers—who are not trained as mental health professionals—to use Collaborative Problem Solving?

Answer: I know that teachers already have a lot of responsibilities. And I know that an astounding number of kids with social, emotional, and behavioral challenges are needlessly slipping through the cracks. I also know that a mental health degree is not a prerequisite for using Collaborative Problem Solving. (Most mental health professionals don't have training in Collaborative Problem Solving, either.) The key qualifications for helping kids with behavioral challenges are an *open mind*, a willingness to *reflect* on one's current practices and see them in a new light, the *courage* to experiment with new practices, and the *patience* and *resolve* to become comfortable assessing lagging skills and unsolved problems and using Plan B.

Question: I was using Plan B with a kid in my class and things seemed to be going well for a few weeks but then deteriorated again. What happened?

Answer: It could be that the solution you and the kid agreed on wasn't as realistic and mutually satisfactory as it originally seemed. That's not your signal to revert back to Plan A. It's your signal to go back to Plan B to figure out why the solution didn't work as well as anticipated and come up with a revised solution.

Question: Are there some challenging kids who are so volatile and unstable that academics should be de-emphasized until things are calmer?

Answer: Yes! Some kids simply aren't "available" for academic learning until they've made headway on the challenges that may be impeding learning. Plunging forward with academics when a kid is bogged down in behavioral challenges is usually an exercise in futility.

Question: Do you ever run into school personnel who refuse to participate in learning about CPS because it goes outside of what they are paid to do?

Answer: Yes, but I find it's much more common that school personnel are willing to go the extra mile to learn about new ways to help kids.

Question: What if Plan B isn't working? What then?

Answer: This is a more interesting question than it might seem, and the answer depends on your definition of the word "working." For many people, "working" refers only to the ultimate destination, the point at which a problem is finally durably solved. But there are many ways in which Plan B is "working" before the ultimate destination is reached. Plan B is working if adults are viewing a kid's difficulties more accurately and more compassionately. It's working if adults are effectively gathering information about a kid's concerns on a given problem and finally achieving an understanding of what's been getting in the kid's way. It's working if the kid is able to listen to adult concerns and take them into account. Plan B is working if the kid is no longer viewing adults as "the enemy." It's working if the kid is participating in discussions about how a given problem can be solved in a way that addresses the concerns of both parties. Plan B is even working if it's not going so well but the kid and adults haven't broken off discussions and are resolved to keep trying.

Question: But are there some students who need more than what can be provided in a general education setting, even if people are using Plan B?

Answer: Yes, there are. But wouldn't it be interesting to see how many students still needed more than what could be provided in general education settings if more general education settings were using Plan B? That aside, there are some kids who need a larger "dose" of Plan B than can be provided in schools and outpatient settings, kids who continue to behave in an unsafe manner at home, at school, and/ or in the community. Many start a downward spiral early, become increasingly alienated, begin exhibiting more serious forms of inappropriate behavior, and begin to hang out with other children who have come down a similar path. After all else has been tried—therapy, medication, perhaps even alternative day-school placements—what many of these kids ultimately need is a change of environment. A new start. A way to start working on a new identity. Once alienation and deviance become a kid's identity and a means of being a part of something, things are a lot harder to turn around. Fortunately, there are some outstanding therapeutic day schools and residential facilities in the United States that do an exceptional job of working with such kids.

12

Better

You've made it to the last chapter, and you've covered a lot of ground on the way. The first goal was to help you view your explosive kid more accurately, beginning with the *kids do well if they can* mentality. You now know that your kid's explosions occur when the demands being placed on him exceed his capacity to respond well, and that if he could respond well he would. We removed from the discussion a lot of the things that are commonly said about explosions (that they're intentional, goal-oriented, and purposeful), explosive kids (that they're unmotivated, attention-seeking, manipulative, button-pushing), and the parents of explosive kids (that they're passive, permissive, and inconsistent disciplinarians). We examined the various lagging skills and unsolved problems that can set the stage for explosions, and your first task was to identify the lagging skills and unsolved problems that applied to your situation. After being introduced to a few explosive kids, you learned why traditional discipline—with its heavy emphasis on rewarding and punishing—may not have improved your situation. You learned about a different way of going about doing things—Plan B—and were encouraged to start *proactively* solving the problems that precipitate explosions in your household. And you read about the different ways in which Plan B can go awry and how to correct those problems.

My hope is that things are now better in your household. If so, there are a lot of factors that could be at work. Sometimes things get better simply because adults understand their explosive kid's difficulties better than they did before. Sometimes things get better because adults have removed some unnecessary demands or expectations from a kid's radar screen (Plan C). Sometimes things are better because adults rely far less on imposing their will—Plan A—in their interactions with their explosive kid. And sometimes things are better because that big pile of unsolved problems that stood next to their kid at the beginning of the book is a lot smaller now because many of the problems were solved—one at a time—with Plan B. Along the way, communication between parents and their kid improved, and so did their relationship. Ideally, things are better because of all of these factors in combination.

Sometimes it's hard to notice that things are getting better. Some adults have a preordained notion of what life is going to be like when things are "finally better" and are disappointed to find when they arrive at "better" that living with their explosive kid still isn't a bowl of cherries. Some wish it weren't so hard to make things better or that it could be accomplished at a faster pace. How quickly progress is achieved and how hard it is differs for every explosive kid and every family. And the definition of "better" is different for every explosive kid and every family, too. So, for what it's worth, here's my definition of better: *it's better.*

Could things be even better than they are now? You'll find out.

And if you're the type of person who likes to read the entire book before putting what you've read into action, your time has come.

Perhaps you're wondering what happened to Jennifer, star of the Waffle Episode, which is where we started, eleven chapters ago. Does she still get pretty frustrated sometimes? Yes. Does she still explode? No.

"I used to spend so much energy being upset . . . then I realized it wasn't doing me any good," she said recently. "Now, if I get upset about something, a lot of times I'll just stop for a second and ask myself if being upset is going to make things any better. I've learned I have a pretty obsessive personality. If I'm upset about something, I can spend a lot of time thinking about it. So I do things that will take my mind off of what I'm upset about."

Jennifer's mother often reflects on the road she and her daughter have traveled together.

"I want people who have a child like Jennifer to know that there is light at the end of the tunnel. The road isn't always easy—even today—but things are far better than we ever thought possible. Jennifer often thanks us for not giving up on her.

"I did have to come to grips with the fact that I didn't get the child I hoped for. And I had to have different priorities for Jennifer. Some things that I thought mattered a lot really didn't matter at all . . . not in the scheme of things . . . not with this child. And I know this is going to sound crazy, but I had to start finding humor in my situation. It's easy to get so wrapped up in the moment. But it's the big picture that matters. I held my family together. My marriage survived. My other kids turned out okay. And Jennifer is a wonderful young woman."

If you've been thinking, "Shouldn't all children be raised this way?" the answer is, "Yes, of course." You see, while the CPS model has its roots in the treatment of explosive kids, it's clear that it's not just explosive kids who benefit from identifying their concerns, having those concerns taken seriously, taking another person's concerns into account, generating and considering alternative solutions to problems, working toward mutually satisfactory solutions, and resolving disputes and disagreements without conflict. It's *all* kids (and all adults).

And, to close, this e-mail a mom sent me recently:

Since my son was two-and-a-half years old, we've been trying to figure him out and help him. Over the years, there have been several different types of evaluations done, and we've been in several different types of treatment, including medicine. Finally, I read The Explosive Child. *THE SUN HAS COME OUT! It's made an enormous difference. We help him (and his sister) be calm and work things out, generate solutions. Within the last two months, my son has really turned a corner, can think, generate solutions, and is less anxious with other kids and more confident in his ability to be with them. He has stopped saying nasty things to us and other kids, and his swearing—which was his version of exploding—has almost disappeared. He wants to please us and has been working really hard to improve himself. He's smart, funny, a great artist, and so loving. It's so great that your approach is letting more of what's great in my son show through more easily. I'd hate for anyone to go through what we've been through. There's so much out there and not much of it is very helpful. I only wish I had read the book years ago.*

Kids do well if they can. Now you know what to do if they can't.

Additional Reading

Problem Solving and Challenging Kids

Gordon, T. *Parent Effectiveness Training: The Proven Program for Raising Responsible Children*. 30th anniversary ed. New York: Three Rivers Press, 2000.

Kurcinka, M. S. *Raising Your Spirited Child: A Guide for Parents Whose Child Is More Intense, Sensitive, Perceptive, Persistent, and Energetic*. Rev. ed. New York: Harper Paperbacks, 2006.

Turecki, S. *The Difficult Child*. Rev. ed. New York: Bantam, 2000.

Waugh, L. D. *Tired of Yelling: Teaching Our Children to Resolve Conflict*. New York: Pocket Books, 2001.

Helping Challenging Kids at School

Greene, R. W. *Lost at School: Why Our Kids with Behavioral Challenges Are Falling Through the Cracks and How We Can Help Them*. New York: Scribner, 2009.

Kohn, A. *Beyond Discipline: From Compliance to Community*. 10th anniversary ed. Alexandria, Va.: Association for Supervision and Curriculum Development, 2006.

Levin, D. E. *Teaching Young Children in Violent Times: Building a Peaceable Classroom*. 2nd ed. Cambridge, Mass.: Educators for Social Responsibility, 2003.

Levin, J., and J. M. Shanken-Kaye. *The Self-Control Classroom: Understanding and Managing the Disruptive Behavior of All Students Including Students with ADHD*. Dubuque, Iowa: Kendall/Hunt Publishing, 2001.

Noddings, N. *The Challenge to Care in Schools: An Alternative Approach to Education*. 2nd ed. New York: Teachers College Press, 2005.

Parent–Teacher Interactions

Lawrence-Lightfoot, S. *The Essential Conversation: What Parents and Teachers Can Learn from Each Other.* New York: Random House, 2003.

Nonverbal Learning Disability

Stewart, K. *Helping a Child with Nonverbal Learning Disorder or Asperger's Syndrome: A Parent's Guide.* 2nd ed. Oakland, Calif.: New Harbinger, 2007.

Social Skills

Nowicki, S., and M. Duke. *Helping the Child Who Doesn't Fit In.* Atlanta, Ga.: Peachtree Publishers, 1992.

Sensory Integration Dysfunction

Kranowitz, C. S. *The Out-of-Sync Child: Recognizing and Coping with Sensory Processing Disorder.* Rev. ed. New York: Perigee, 2006.

Sibling Issues

Faber, A., and E. Mazlish. *Siblings Without Rivalry: How to Help Your Children Live Together So You Can Live Too*. New York: HarperCollins, 2004.

Psychopharmacology

Koplewicz, H. *It's Nobody's Fault: New Hope and Help for Difficult Children and Their Parents*. New York: Three Rivers Press, 1997.

For more information and resources on the Collaborative Problem Solving approach, visit www.explosivechild.com.

Index

accountability, of child, 142
adaptability
    children's preference for,
        39–40
    as lagging skill, 12–14
ADHD (attention-deficit/hyper-
    activity disorder), 6–7, 16,
    50, 247
adults. *See* parents; teachers
advice-giving, 156
affect, separation of, 28–35
after-school activities, 155–160,
    274–275
aggression, physical and verbal
    as characteristic of explosive
        children, 2–3, 5, 8, 16, 78
    communication skills and, 27–28

differences between other chil-
    dren and explosive children, 8
examples of, 59–60
agitation
    frustration tolerance and, 30
    in fueling explosiveness, 31–32
allowance money, 74, 127–128
alternative medicine, 204
ambiguity, difficulty handling,
    35–37, 54–57, 58–62, 210–211
antidepressants, 30–31, 58, 176, 178
antihypertensives, 63
antipsychotics, 30, 178
anxiety
    in fueling explosiveness, 32
    as impedance to problem solv-
        ing, 28–35, 50–52, 58–62

anxiety (*cont.*)
  managing, 32–35
  overcoming, 34–35
  perfectionism and, 237–238
aripiprazole (Abilify), 178
Asperger's disorder, 16
assessment mechanisms
  high-stakes testing and, 255
  in schools, 64–65, 259–260
Assessment of Language Skills
    and Unsolved Problems
    (ALSUP), 260
atomoxetine (Strattera), 177
attention, clichés concerning
    need for, 40
attention-deficit/hyperactivity
    disorder (ADHD), 6–7, 16,
    50, 247
attitude, clichés concerning, 42
atypical antipsychotics, 178
autism spectrum disorders, 36

babies, frustrations and inflexi-
    bility of, 13
bad attitudes, clichés concerning,
    42
bad choices, clichés concerning,
    41–42
battle picking, 112–113
bedtime
  adult concerns and, 102
  Plan B and, 98, 99, 102
  transition to, 29–30, 44
behavior, reasons for maladaptive,
    16–18
behavior management, 3, 14–15
  parental reactions to, 75
  *See also specific strategy or inter-
    vention*

belief system, inaccuracy of exist-
    ing, 201, 203
bipolar disorder, 2–3, 7, 16, 50
black-and-white thinking, 35–37,
    50–52
boredom, 44
bullying, 31, 270
button-pushing, clichés concern-
    ing, 42, 73

catastrophizing, 239
chemical factor in explosions,
    253
children
  deciding to use medications
    with, 178–179, 203–204
  individuality of, 39–40, 276–277
  planned/willful behavior of,
    207–208
  See also "kids do well if they can
    philosophy; explosive children"
chores, 44
class assignments, 44
classmates, interactions with, 44
classrooms
  inclusion and, 253
  See also school; teachers
cleaning room, 44
clothing
  labels on, 50
  sensory hypersensitivities and,
    44, 50
coaching, implementing Plan B in
    schools, 260–261
cognitive skills
  black-and-white thinking,
    35–37, 50–52, 194–195
  characteristics of explosive
    child, 7

disorganization in, 25
reflexive negativity and, 25–26
separation of affect, 28–35
shifting cognitive set, 5–7,
    35–37, 54–57, 58–62
See also flexibility; problem
    solving
Collaborative Problem Solving
    (CPS), 84, 89–92, 100–101,
    235–236, 253, 257, 283–285
See also Plan B
communication patterns, 234–244
    catastrophizing, 239
    dwelling on the past, 239
    examples of, 240–244
    interrupting, 239, 241
    lecturing, 239
    mind reading, 234–236, 244
    perfectionism, 237–238
    put-downs, 239
    sarcasm, 239, 242–243
    speculation, 234–236
    talking through a third person,
        239
communication skills
    communication patterns within
        families, 234–244
    difficulty expressing concerns,
        needs, or thoughts in words,
        26–28, 54–57
    difficulty in communicating,
        27–28, 181–189
    encouraging communication,
        134
    examples of problems with,
        27–28
    pictures and, 183–184, 185–186
    working with extremely lim-
        ited, 183–184

computers, screen time and,
    43–44, 98, 155–160
concerns
    adult, 102–103
    adult not believing child's,
        138–139
    child not caring about adult,
        139–140
    in Define the Problem step of
        Plan B, 117–118, 126–128,
        143, 145
    difficulty expressing in words,
        26–28, 54–57, 183–184
    about specific problems, 100–
        101
    See also specific problem
Concerta (methylphenidate), 177
concrete thinking, 35–37
consequences, 71–81
    at school, 255–257, 278, 280–281
    See also reward/punishment
conventional wisdom, 14–17, 19
co-parenting, 58–62, 244–245
CPS. *See* Collaborative Problem
    Solving (CPS); Plan B
crankiness, frustration tolerance
    and, 30

Define the Problem step, 100–104
    for black-and-white thinkers,
        195
    concerns about specific prob-
        lems, 100–101
    described, 90, 117
    in Emergency Plan B, 115
    initiating, 117–118, 126–128,
        143, 145
    in Proactive Plan B, 103–104,
        115, 188

Define the Problem Step (*cont.*)
See also specific problem
demands
  expectations and, 113
  explosions related to, 46,
    55–56, 59–62
  nature of, 23–24
  Plan A and, 84–85
  skills to deal with, 45
  transitions and, 29–30
depression, 7
developmental age, 212
developmental delays, 14, 15,
    31–32
  See also lagging skills
dexmethylphenidate (Focalin),
    177
diagnosis
  of explosive children, 5–8, 15–16
  limitations of, 179
  of mood disorders (bipolar dis-
    order and depression), 30–31,
    58, 63
disagreements, unevenness of
  skills development in working
  out, 12–14
disappointment, problems handling, 45
disapproval, 56, 143. *See also*
  Plan A
discipline
  differences between other chil-
    dren and explosive children, 8
  need for different approaches
    to, 8
  parents as poor disciplinarians,
    14–15, 73–74
  school programs, 253
  transforming school, 262

understanding explosive chil-
    dren, 14–15
disorganization
  lagging skills and, 24–26
  reflexive negativity and, 25–26
dispute resolution, between sib-
    lings, 225–233
distractibility, medications for,
    176, 177
drilling process, 95–100
  in cotton candy problem, 168–
    170
  example of, 96–98
  homework problem and, 135–
    138
  nature of, 95
  perseverance in, 135–136
  problems with, 135–138
  sensory hypersensitivities and,
    136, 137–138
  what not to do in, 98–100
dueling solutions, Plan B and, 100
Dunn, Kari, 186
dwelling on the past, 239

educated guessing
  example of, 132–135
  nature of, 131–132
embarrassment factor, 4, 191–
    192, 213, 252–253
Emergency Plan B
  define the problem step, 115
  described, 90–91, 117
  Empathy step, 114–115, 187–188
  examples, 165–173
  Plan C versus, 147–148
  Proactive Plan B versus, 114–
    115, 121–122, 170–173
  in school, 263–265, 275–276

emotion regulation skills, 12–14
  difficulty managing emotional
    response to frustration,
    28–35, 50–52, 54–57, 58–62
  separation of affect, 28–35
emotions
  vocabulary of feelings and, 184
  See also emotion regulation skills
Empathy step
  for black-and-white thinkers,
    194–195
  described, 90, 100, 117
  drilling and, 95–100, 135–138
  educated guessing and, 131–132
  in Emergency Plan B, 114–115,
    187–188
  failure to enter, 131–135
  identifying unsolved problems
    in, 50–54, 182–183
  information gathering in, 91–92
  initiating, 117–118, 124–125,
    144–145, 210
  in Proactive Plan B, 92–93,
    114–115, 121, 187–188
  reflective listening in, 115
  "What's up?" and, 92–95, 117–
    118
  See also reassurance; specific
    problem
Essential Conversation, The (Lawrence-Lightfoot), 271
explanations for explosions,
  13–15, 16–18
  See also conventional wisdom
explosions
  description/characteristics of,
    2–3, 5, 16
  embarrassment factor in, 252–
    253
explanations for, 13–15, 16–18
at home versus at school, 213,
  251–253
impact on family, 3, 7–8
predictability of, 45, 91, 279
reasons for, 16–18
explosive children
  characteristics of, 2–3, 5–8, 16
  clichés concerning, 40–43
  compared with other children,
    5–8
  difficulties of, 16–18
  as embarrassment to parents, 4
  explanation for behavior of,
    13–15, 16–18
  failure to progress developmen-
    tally, 13–15, 31–32
  fear of family members toward,
    3–4
  misconceptions concerning,
    40–43
  misdiagnosing, 5–8, 15–16
  understanding, 7–8, 13–19,
    21–22
  See also specific problem
extrinsic motivation, 77

Faber, Adele, 233
facilitators
  parents as, 226–233
  teachers as, 269–270
family, 221–250
  communication patterns with,
    234–244
  disagreements within, 221
  grandparents, 244–245
  impact of explosions on, 3, 7–8
  See also parents; siblings of ex-
    plosive children

fatigue, frustration tolerance and,
30
flexibility
developmental delays and, 31
identifying factors compromising skills of, 21–22
as lagging skill, 12–13, 17, 18,
19, 35–37
See also inflexibility
fluoxetine (Prozac), 66, 178
Focalin (dexmethylphenidate), 177
food, 44
picky eating, 87–88
Plan C and, 87–88
sensory hypersensitivities and,
50, 136, 137–138
shifting gears and, 55–56
transition to meal time, 59–60,
62, 139–140
friends, 3
Plan B and, 97–98, 99
See also social skills
frustration tolerance
of babies, 13
characteristics of explosive children, 2, 5–8, 6–7
as critical skill, 17, 19
description of difficulties by explosive children, 17, 18, 19
developmental delays and, 31
difficulty managing emotional
response to frustration,
28–35, 50–52, 54–57, 58–62
explosive children compared to
other children, 5–8
factors compromising skills of,
21–22
as lagging skill, 12–13, 17, 18,
19, 24–26, 28–35, 50–52

onset of, 13
of parents, 16–18
understanding explosive children, 15
See also specific problem

"genius" role, 105–106, 133–134,
140, 182, 211
grandparents, 244–245
Gray, Carol, 186
grilling process, 95
grounding, 14, 74
group discussions, 269–270

high-stakes testing, 255
home
explosions at school versus,
213, 251–253
list of unsolved problems, 44
homeopathy, 204
homework problem, 44
adult concerns and, 102
communication patterns and,
236–237, 238
drilling and, 135–138
examples of, 106–111, 170–173
Plan A and, 85–86
Plan B and, 96–97, 100, 102,
271–275
in Proactive Plan B, 103–104
transitions and, 22–23, 124–126
writing and, 272–273
honesty, 139–140
household chores, 44
hyperactivity, 4, 141
medications for, 141, 176–178
See also ADHD (attention-
deficit/hyperactivity disorder)
hypothesis testing, 131–132, 133

"I don't care," meanings of, 135
"I don't know," meanings of, 132–135
ignoring, as strategy for managing behavior, 5
imposing will. *See* Plan A
impulsiveness
    lagging skills and, 24–26, 50–52
    medications for, 176–178
inattention, medications for, 177
incentives. *See* reward/punishment
inclusion model, 253
infants
    difficult, 13
    temperament of, 13
inflexibility
    of babies, 13
    as characteristic of explosive children, 3, 5–6, 7
    as learning disability, 15
    onset of, 13
    of parents, 79
    reciprocal, 87–88, 254
    See also flexibility
insisting, as strategy for managing behavior, 5
intermittent explosive disorder, 2–3
interrupting, 239, 241
interventions, explanations as guiding, 13–15, 19
Invitation step, 104–112
    for black-and-white thinkers, 195
    described, 90, 117
    initiating, 145–147
    mutually satisfactory solutions in, 106–112, 138–140, 149–150, 284
    nature of, 104

in Proactive Plan B, 188–189
purpose of collaboration, 104–105
realistic solutions in, 106–112, 148–150, 284
irrationality
    in fueling explosiveness, 32
    See also rational thinking
irritability
    frustration tolerance and, 30
    in fueling explosiveness, 31–32
    as impedance to problem solving, 28–35, 50–52, 58–62
    medications for, 176

"kids do well if they can" philosophy, 11–19, 151–173
    adaptive versus maladaptive behavior and, 39–41
    basic premise of, 15
    identification of pathways, 21–22
    rewards/punishment and, 75, 206
    understanding of explosive children, 13–19
    unevenness of skills development, 11–14

labeling, 2–3
    and explanations as guiding interventions, 14–15
    mental illness and, 42–43
    See also diagnosis
lagging skills, 22–43
    chronic irritability or anxiety impeding problem solving, 28–35, 50–52, 58–62
    difficulty adapting to changes in plan or new rules, 58–62

lagging skills (*cont.*)

difficulty appreciating impact of behavior on others, 50–52

difficulty considering likely outcomes or consequences, 24–26

difficulty considering range of solutions, 24–26, 50–51, 58–62

difficulty deviating from rules or routines, 35–37, 54–57, 58–62

difficulty expressing concerns, needs, or thoughts in words, 26–28, 54–57, 183–184

difficulty handling transitions, 22–24, 29–30, 50–52, 62, 124–126

difficulty handling unpredictability, ambiguity, uncertainty, or novelty, 35–37, 54–57, 58–62, 210–211

difficulty managing emotional response to frustration, 28–35, 50–52, 54–57, 58–62

difficulty reflecting on multiple thoughts or ideas, 24–26

difficulty seeing "grays," 35–37, 50–52

difficulty shifting from original idea or solution, 5–7, 35–37, 54–57, 58–62

difficulty taking into account situational factors, 35–37, 54–57

identifying, 45, 47, 259–260

list of, 38–39

nature of, 21

and parent-teacher problem solving, 271

participation in Plan B and, 190–195

Plan B as framework for approach to teach lagging skills, 196–203

Proactive Plan B and, 199–201

in school, 259–260

See also flexibility; frustration tolerance; problem solving

language processing skills, 141

examples of problems with, 27–28

See also swearing problem

Lawrence-Lightfoot, Sarah, 271

lecturing, 239

Lexapro, 178

limit-setting, 3, 8, 142–143

lisdexamfetamine (Vyvanse), 177

lithium carbonate, 66

logic, in problem solving, 28–35

lying, 214–216

mainstreaming, 253

manipulation, clichés concerning, 41, 73

Mazlish, Elaine, 233

medications, 176–181

alternative medicine and, 204

antidepressants, 30, 58, 176, 178

antihypertensives, 63

antipsychotics, 30, 178

characteristics of prescribing doctors, 179–180

chemical factor in explosions and, 253

deciding to use with children, 178–179, 203–204

discretion concerning, 132–133, 180–181
effectiveness of, 74
hyperactivity and, 141, 176–178
length of time on, 203–204
negative reactions to using, 176–177
problems taking, 44, 132–133, 180–181
side effects of, 178–179, 180
stimulants, 30, 177–178, 213
as strategy for managing behavior, 5, 72–73
taking at school, 132–133, 180–181
See also specific medications
mental illness, clichés concerning, 42–43
mentality, implementing Plan B in schools, 258
methylphenidate (Concerta; Ritalin), 58, 177
mind reading, 234–236, 244
mood disorders (bipolar disorder and depression)
diagnosing, 30–31, 58, 63
medications for, 176–178
misdiagnosing, 30–31
morning routine, 44
motivation
clichés concerning, 41
extrinsic, 77
"kids do well if they can" philosophy and, 206
See also reward/punishment
mutually satisfactory solutions, 106–112, 138–140, 149–150, 284

nagging. See demands
name-calling, 197–199
needs, difficulty expressing in words, 26–28, 54–57, 183–184
negativity, reflexive, 25–26
novelty, difficulty handling, 35–37, 54–57, 58–62, 210–211
nurturing, as strategy for managing behavior, 5

objectivity, in problem solving, 28–35
obsessiveness, medications for, 176
one-upmanship, 242–243
oppositional-defiant disorder, 2–3, 16
overgeneralization, 237

parenting
good, 46
ineffectiveness of conventional, 19
parents
assumptions of, 105–106
behavior of, 8
blaming selves, 14, 73–74, 245
characteristics of, 8
co-parenting arrangements and, 58–62, 244–245
disapproval of child's behavior, 56, 143. See also Plan A
divorce and, 58–62
explosive child as embarrassment to, 4, 46
as facilitators with siblings, 226–233

parents (*cont.*)
fear of child by, 3–4
frustrations of, 16–18
"genius" role and, 105–106,
133–134, 140, 182, 211
inflexibility of, 79
parent-teacher problem solving,
271–275
as poor disciplinarians, 14–15,
73–74
pressures on marriage, 245–
247
reactions to behavior management programs, 75
reactions to explosive child,
1–5
splitting by child and, 248–249
strains on, 3–5, 17–19
See also family; parenting
pathways, identifying, 21–22
perfectionism, 237–238
perseverance
in drilling process, 135–136
implementing Plan B in schools,
262
picky eating, 87–88
pictures
communication skills and, 183–
184, 185–186
in problem-solving binder, 185–
186
Plan A, 84–86
"clever" form of, 106
comparison with Plan B and
Plan C, 106, 111, 112–113,
120–121, 123–124, 127–128,
168, 249
decreasing use of, 205
described, 290

effectiveness of, 84–85, 248,
249–250
examples of, 209
limitations of, 85
limit-setting in, 142–143
nature of, 84–85, 113–114, 116
paradox of, 85–86
in the real world, 143–144
reducing use of, 175
role in causing explosions, 177
in school, 213
siblings responding to, 249–250
"who's boss" approach and,
85–86
Plan B, 89–112
adjusting for compromised
communication skills, 181–
182
avoiding use of, 120–121
best time to use, 90–91
challenges of working with, 111,
219, 285–286
"Cheat Sheet," 118
"clever" form of Plan A versus,
106
communication problems and,
181–189
comparison with Plan A and
Plan C, 106, 111, 112–113,
123, 124, 127–128, 168, 249–
250
complications with, 154–160
as default option, 148
Define the Problem step. *See*
Define the Problem step
described, 290
disapproval step in, 143
Emergency. *See* Emergency
Plan B

Empathy step. *See* Empathy step

as framework for approach to teach lagging skills, 196–203

implementing at school, 257–262

increasing use of, 205

interactions between siblings and, 223–224

Invitation step. *See* Invitation step

language of, 151–152. *See also* "kids do well if they can" philosophy

as last resort, 122

learning, 118

length of time on, 204–205

limit-setting in, 142–143

nature of, 84, 89–90, 116

with preordained solution, 123

Proactive. *See* Proactive Plan B

refusal to learn about, 247–248

rewarding child for participating in, 206

for safety issues, 144–147, 190–195

skills taught by participating in, 190–195

three steps/ingredients, 117, 123–124, 149

time required for, 148

Plan B Flowchart, 261

Plan C, 86–89

comparison with Plan A and Plan B, 106, 111, 112–113, 120–121, 123–124, 127–128, 168, 249

described, 290

Emergency Plan B versus, 147–148

"giving in" versus, 86–87

increasing use of, 205

"momentary," 275–276

nature of, 84, 86, 114, 116

"Proactive," 275

reducing use of, 175

in school, 262–265

point systems, 14, 74

described, 51, 78–79

limitations of, 51

power struggles, 15, 29–30, 100

practice, implementing Plan B in schools, 260–261

predictability of explosions, 45, 91, 279. *See also* routines; unpredictability

prescribing doctors, characteristics of, 179–180

Proactive Plan B

applying, 119–121, 155–160, 181–182

for child with extremely limited communication skills, 183–184

Define the Problem step, 103–104, 115, 188

described, 91, 117

difficulty participating in, 115–116

effectiveness of, 165

Emergency Plan B versus, 114–115, 121–122, 170–173

Empathy step, 92–93, 114–115, 121, 187–188

identifying solutions, 185–189

implementing in schools, 258–259

Proactive Plan B (*cont.*)
  initiating, 141
  Invitation step in, 188–189
  lagging skills and, 199–201
  in parent-teacher problem solving, 271–275
  "seamless," 152–154
  selecting solutions, 185–189
  for siblings, 225–226
  student-teacher problem solving and, 262–263
problems
  concerns about specific, 100–101
  generic problem vocabulary, 184–185
  See also Define the Problem step; problem solving; *specific problem*
problems in living, 42–43
problem solving
  anxiety and, 28–35, 50–52, 58–62
  as critical skill, 17, 19
  developmental delays and, 31
  difficulty considering range of solutions, 24–26, 50–51, 58–62
  difficulty expressing concerns, needs, or thoughts in words and, 26–27
  disappointing solutions in, 211–212
  general set of solutions, 187
  group discussions, 269–270
  irritability as impedance to, 28–35, 50–52, 58–62
  as lagging skill, 12–14, 17–19, 24–26, 50–52. *See also* unsolved problems

  parent-teacher, 271–275
  problem-solving binder and, 186
  realistic solutions and, 106–112, 148–150, 284
  specific solutions in, 186–187
  student-student, 266–269
  student-teacher, 262–265
  understanding of explosive children, 15
  See also Collaborative Problem Solving (CPS); solutions; unsolved problems; *specific problem*
problem-solving binder, 185–186
Problem-Solving Team, 92, 105, 140
Prozac (fluoxetine), 66, 178
psychoeducational evaluation, 64–65
psychologizing, 234–236
put-downs, 239

rational thinking
  in problem solving, 28–35
  See also irrationality
reactive attachment disorder, 16
realistic solutions, 106–112, 148–150, 284
reasoning, as strategy for managing behavior, 5
reassurance
  offering, 134
  as strategy for managing behavior, 5
  See also specific problem
reciprocal inflexibility, 87–88, 254
redirecting, as strategy for managing behavior, 5

reflective listening, 115
reflexive negativity, 25–26
remedial assistance, 12
remorse, of explosive children, 79–80
residual heat, 121–122
responsibility, of child, 142
reward/punishment
    accountability of child and, 142
    alternatives to, 75–76
    bad attitude and, 42
    effectiveness of, 75–76, 77
    formal programs, 3, 76–77, 78
    "kids do well if they can" philosophy and, 75, 206
    limitations of, 28, 77, 78–80
    parents as poor disciplinarians, 14–15
    for participating in Plan B, 206
    as strategy for managing behavior, 3, 5
    understanding explosive children, 14–15
    See also consequences; motivation; point systems; time-out; specific problem
rigidity, 35–37
    characteristics of explosive children, 3, 5–6
Risperdal (risperidone), 178
risperidone (Risperdal), 178
Ritalin (methylphenidate), 58, 177
routines
    difficulty deviating from, 35–37, 54–57, 58–62
    See also predictability of explosions; unpredictability

rubrics, 255
rules
    difficulty adapting to new, 58–62
    difficulty deviating from, 35–37, 54–57, 58–62

safety issues
    Plan B for, 144–147, 190–195
    at school, 277–283
sarcasm, 239, 242–243
school, 251–287
    assessment mechanisms, 64–65, 259–260
    behavior problems at, 177
    consequences at, 255–257, 278, 280–281
    discipline programs, 253
    embarrassment factor and, 213
    Emergency Plan B and, 263–265, 275–276
    emphasis on academics in, 284–285
    examples of difficulties, 51–52, 57, 63–68, 253–254
    explosions at home versus, 213, 251–253
    group discussions, 269–270
    high-stakes testing, 255
    inclusion model and, 253
    lagging skills in, 259–260
    list of unsolved problems, 44–45
    parent-teacher problem solving, 271–275
    Plan A and, 213
    Plan B and, 257–262
    Plan C and, 262–265
    safety issues, 277–283

school (*cont.*)
  student-student problem solving, 266–269
  student-teacher problem solving, 262–265
  taking medications at, 132–133, 180–181
  unsolved problems in, 44–45, 259–260
  zero-tolerance policies, 255
  See also teachers
school resistance
  adult concerns and, 102
  example of, 201–203
  Plan B and, 97, 98, 102
seeing the big picture, 36–37
selective serotonin re-uptake inhibitors (SSRI antidepressants), 178
sensory hypersensitivities, 44, 50–54, 136, 137–138
shifting cognitive set, 5–7, 35–37, 54–57, 58–62
shifting gears
  difficulty adapting to changes in plan or new rules, 58–62
  difficulty shifting from original idea or solution, 35–37, 54–57, 58–62
siblings of explosive children, 1–3, 13, 14, 44, 222–233
  dispute resolution between, 225–233
  Emergency Plan B for, 225–226
  empathy in working with, 223, 224–225
  fairness and, 160–165
  interactions with explosive children, 222–223

parents as facilitators with, 226–233
  Plan B and, 223–224
  Proactive Plan B for, 225–226
  protecting, 222–223
  responding to Plan A, 249–250
  responding to Plan B, 249–250
  sharing problem and, 226–233
Siblings Without Rivalry (Faber and Mazlish), 233
side effects, of medications, 178–179, 180
silence, in Empathy step of Plan B, 131
situational factor in explosions, 35–37, 54–57, 252
skills
  unevenness in development of, 11–14
  See also lagging skills; pathways; *specific skills*
social skills
  communication in. *See* communication skills
  interaction with classmates, 44
  sharing problem, 199–201
  See also friends
solutions
  Plan B and, 100
  See also problem solving
speculation, 234–236
splitting, 248–249
SSRI antidepressants, 178
sticker charts, 3, 14, 25–26, 72, 74
stimulants, 30, 177–178, 213
strategies. *See* conventional wisdom; interventions

Strattera (atomoxetine), 177
student-student problem solving, 266–269
student-teacher problem solving, 262–263
surprises, difficulty handling, 35–37, 54–57
swearing, 7
  difficulty expressing concerns, needs, or thoughts in words and, 26
  examples of, 26, 58–60
  Plan B for, 198–199, 224–225
  teaching lagging skills and, 196–199

talking through a third person, 239
teachers
  expectations for children, 276–277
  as facilitators of group problem solving, 269–270
  interactions with, 44
  parent-teacher problem solving, 271–275
  student-teacher problem solving in schools, 262–265
teaching skills, 189–203
  skills taught by participating in Plan B, 190–195
teasing, 270
television, screen time and, 43–44, 155–160
temperament, difficult, 13
thoughts
  difficulty expressing in words, 26–28, 54–57, 183–184
  See also cognitive skills

tics, 7, 63–68
time, implementing Plan B in schools, 258–259
time-out, 3, 14
  limitations of, 25–26, 55–56, 72
  pros and cons of, 207
  using, 78–79
Tourette's disorder, 7, 63–68
transitions
  difficulty handling, 22–24, 29–30, 50–52, 62, 124–126
  signs of difficulties with, 23–24
trust
  of child by parents, 190–193
  lying and, 214–216
  problems with, 65–68

uncertainty, difficulty handling, 35–37, 54–57, 58–62, 210–211
unpredictability
  characteristics of explosive children, 7–8
  difficulty handling, 35–37, 54–57, 58–62
  explosive children compared with other children, 7–8
  See also predictability of explosions
unsolved problems, 17–19, 24–26, 43–46
  difficulty navigating, 76–77
  examples of, 44–45, 53, 57, 62
  explosions and information about, 147–148
  at home, 44

unsolved problems (*cont.*)
  identifying, 45, 47, 50–54, 182–185, 259–260
  medication and, 31
  and parent-teacher problem solving, 271
  at school, 44–45, 259–260
  and *who, what, where,* and *when* or explosive outbursts, 43–44, 53, 95

video games
  adult concerns and, 102
  Plan B and, 97–98, 102
vocabulary
  difficulty expressing concerns, needs, or thoughts in words, 26–28, 54–57
  for feelings, 184
  generic problem, 184–185
  See also language processing skills; words
Vyvanse (lisdexamfetamine), 177

waking up, 44
  adult concerns and, 102
  Plan B and, 98, 99, 102
"What's up?"
  drilling and, 95
  in Empathy step, 92–95, 117–118
  example of use, 96–100
  meanings of, 94–95
  silence as response to, 94–95
"who's boss" approach, 15, 29–30, 81, 85–86, 90
words
  difficulty expressing concerns, needs, or thoughts in, 26–28, 54–57, 183–184
  extremely limited communication skills and, 183–184
  see also vocabulary
working things out with child. *See* Collaborative Problem Solving (CPS); Plan B

zero-tolerance policies, 255